CREATING THE
ANYWHERE, ANYTIME
CLASSROOM

A **BLUEPRINT** for **LEARNING**
ONLINE in Grades K–12

CASEY **REASON**

LISA **REASON**

CRYSTAL **GUILER**

Solution Tree | Press

a division of
Solution Tree

555 North Morton Street
Bloomington, IN 47404
800.733.6786 (toll free) / 812.336.7700
FAX: 812.336.7790

email: info@SolutionTree.com
SolutionTree.com

Visit **go.SolutionTree.com/technology** to access materials related to this book.

Printed in the United States of America

21   20   19   18   17   1   2   3   4   5

Library of Congress Cataloging-in-Publication Data

Names: Reason, Casey S., author. | Reason, Lisa, author. | Guiler, Crystal,

    author.

Title: Creating the anywhere, anytime classroom : a blueprint for learning

    online in grades K-12 / authors: Casey Reason, Lisa Reason, and Crystal

    Guiler.

Description: Bloomington, IN : Solution Tree Press, [2017] | Includes

    bibliographical references and index.

Identifiers: LCCN 2016051541 | ISBN 9781943874866 (perfect bound)

Subjects: LCSH: Computer assisted instruction--Curricula--Planning.

Classification: LCC LB1028.5 .R338 2017 | DDC 371.33--dc23 LC record available at https://lccn.loc.
gov/2016051541

Solution Tree

Jeffrey C. Jones, CEO
Edmund M. Ackerman, President

Solution Tree Press

President and Publisher: Douglas M. Rife
Editorial Director: Sarah Payne-Mills
Managing Production Editor: Caroline Weiss
Senior Production Editor: Todd Brakke
Senior Editor: Amy Rubenstein
Proofreader: Evie Madsen
Text and Cover Designer: Laura Cox
Editorial Assistants: Jessi Finn and Kendra Slayton

*For Alexandra, Brice, and Kiah. In an anywhere,
anytime world, choose wisely and never stop
learning, growing, and sharing with others
the gifts God has given you.*

Acknowledgments

We would like to thank the University of Toledo for its ongoing support for the Center for the Advancement of Professional Learning Communities and Virtual Collaboration. The College of Education Dean, Dr. Virginia Kyle, and the College of Distance Learning Dean, Dr. Barbara Kopp Miller, also provided ongoing encouragement and support throughout this process. We would also like to acknowledge the leadership of Dr. Segun Eubanks, Dr. Barbara Hopkins, Brandy Bixler, and Moira Saucedo from the National Education Association. Your leadership in building and developing the NEA's Ed Communities, the largest free digital learning platform in the United States, gave us access to a nation of high-performing teachers who make a difference every day for the students they serve.

Solution Tree Press would like to thank the following reviewers:

James Kapptie
Director of Instructional Technology
Park County School District 6
Cody, Wyoming

Sean Nash
District Online Learning Coordinator
    (eCampus)
North Kansas City School District
Kansas City, Missouri

Sherwin Salomon
Curriculum Specialist
Florida Virtual School
Orlando, Florida

Odalis Q. Tavares
Doctoral Student
Nova Southeastern University
Tampa, Florida

Jennifer Whiting
Director of Product Development
Florida Virtual School
Orlando, Florida

Table of Contents

About the Authors

Casey Reason, PhD, is the director of the Center for the Advancement of Professional Learning Communities and Virtual Collaboration for the University of Toledo. An expert in leadership, school improvement, virtual learning, and the professional learning community (PLC) process, Casey's mission is to help support sustainable reform in education by using PLCs in conjunction with modern-day applications of technology and emerging brain science. A former urban high school principal and central office administrator, Casey has worked with school leaders all over the world to improve the academic achievement of the learners they serve. He has published numerous books, and his publications have been endorsed by best-selling authors Ken Blanchard and Charlotte Danielson. In 2016, he coauthored *Professional Communities at Work and Virtual Collaboration* with transformational thought leader Richard DuFour. Casey is also a distance-learning designer and strategist, winning the 2010 Blackboard International Course Designer of the Year award, a recognition featured on Forbes.com. He also works with Solution Tree's online digital courses and is the developer of the BEST digital leadership solution, a one-of-a-kind leadership and school improvement digital network serving school leaders from all over the world. He and his twin sons Brice and Kiah live in Scottsdale, Arizona.

To learn more about Casey's work, visit his website www.caseyreason.com, or follow @CaseyReason on Twitter.

Lisa Reason, PhD, has been teaching and designing digital graduate curricula for over twelve years. She has successfully led the development and design of numerous masters and doctoral programs and is widely recognized as an expert in online learning. Lisa was the recipient of a doctoral honorarium in 2011 for distinguished faculty and outstanding instructional practice by Grand Canyon University. She was also the recipient of four separate honorariums from Capella University for excellence in scholarship and significant contributions to professional practice. Lisa has been a featured presenter at several scholarly and practitioner-based conferences and has chaired numerous dissertations and research initiatives on topics related to digital learning, instructional practice, leadership, and school reform. Lisa resides in Scottsdale, Arizona, with her twin son Brice and Kiah.

To learn more about Lisa's work, follow @LisaReason1 on Twitter.

Crystal Guiler, as a facilitator, coach, district administrator, curriculum specialist, lead curriculum developer, instructional designer, and virtual learning project manager, has been a leader in K–12 digital learning for over ten years. Crystal has worked extensively with Florida Virtual School, the largest provider of K–12 digital education in the United States. She has developed over seventy higher education and K–12 digital courses and has supervised the development of hundreds of additional digital training solutions.

To book Casey Reason, Lisa Reason, or Crystal Guiler for professional development, contact pd@SolutionTree.com.

Tools and the Master Craftsman

We wrote this book to help educators enhance student learning in the digital age. We recognize that the technology tools that teachers have at their fingertips today are transformational; however, let's be clear, it's not about the new tools. It never will be. It's about teachers finding and choosing new tools, and then learning to skillfully use them. When the teacher learns to use these tools, the tools then become an expression of his or her teaching craft. Over time, the teacher transforms his or her approach to supporting the learning process.

We chose the title *Creating the Anywhere, Anytime Classroom* because, over the last several years, it has become clear to us that distance learning approaches have created viable alternatives to many traditional classrooms. Perhaps even more important is that we realize the benefits and opportunities associated with distance learning for transforming the traditional classroom in dynamic ways. Indeed, the master craftsmen who are teaching our students today have the tools to create viable learning experiences anywhere and anytime. To help put these amorphous new learning opportunities in context, let's examine what we mean by traditional learning, online learning, and blended learning.

Traditional Learning, Online Learning, and Blended Learning—*A Monstrous Mash*

There are some simple definitions that will help you understand the similarities and differences between the following instructional archetypes.

- **Traditional learning:** For the purposes of this book, traditional learning refers to flesh-and-bone, face-to-face teaching and learning experiences that most of us grew up with in K–12 education. They are synchronous in that everyone has to be in the same room at the same time to make the learning experience happen for everyone (Al-Qahtani & Higgins, 2012).

- **Online learning:** Online learning refers to learning experiences that are hosted on a digital platform (Al-Qahtani & Higgins, 2012). If you attend Stanford Online High School (https://ohs.stanford.edu), all of your classes are hosted in a digital platform. Much of your interaction is asynchronous, meaning that interactions don't have to occur all at the same place or at the same time. The teacher posts content, video lectures, and so on, and learners engage with one another in asynchronous, threaded discussion questions. This high school also has synchronous meetings wherein teachers and students all connect on Skype at an agreed-on time each day and hold class, with the teachers leading synchronous conversations and activities. The differentiator is that the learning experiences are online.

- **Blended learning:** A blended learning approach is one wherein teachers deliver instruction in a traditional setting with ongoing, robust learning opportunities simultaneously taking place, with the same group of students, in a digital, online environment. Stanford Online High School holds weeklong, in-person seminars throughout the year. Although the main element of instruction is delivered online, technically the inclusion of these face-to-face learning opportunities makes it a blended learning experience (Picciano & Seaman, 2009).

As you think about your own teaching and learning situation you may recognize that the lines between traditional and online learning are increasingly blurry. Many traditional classrooms today have established parallel, digital learning spaces that allow teachers to post content, stay connected, ask questions, and even create a dialogue with students. The significant advancements in video capacity allow even the most asynchronous digital learning experiences to use a camera to make a personal connection and host an online learning event.

What does this mean for teachers? What does it mean for the profession? In a word—opportunity! The strategies we discuss in this book are designed to meet this wonderfully exciting, amorphous mash of opportunity at our fingertips, and to learn to better understand and harness this amazing power. To do so, we use this book to put these opportunities into an appropriate context. Let's begin by defining digitally enhanced learning.

Digitally Enhanced Learning

There has been quite an evolution in the verbiage educators and students use regarding digital learning. Unfortunately, many of the past phrases don't help us to ascend to our highest aspirations. The phrase *teaching online* speaks to the actions of the instructor and references a ubiquitous teaching platform. *Distance learning* is a phrase that correctly puts the focus on learning, but by emphasizing the word *distance*, it suggests that this is a method of learning that exists only as a simple, convenient alternative to traditional live classroom instruction. It also has the side effect of leaving blended classrooms out of the equation.

Digital learning, an increasingly accepted term in the teaching community, represents the strategic application of an endless array of technological tools to support the learning process (Selwyn, 2011). This could include online platforms, apps, and other web-based assets (Kong et al., 2014). Note that although there are assistive digital tools, including a variety of learning apps, designed to function offline in a physical classroom, in this book we focus specifically on digital tools that help facilitate learning while online.

Throughout this book, we use the term *digitally enhanced learning* (DEL) to describe the strategic use of digital tools and various virtual learning platforms to support and enhance the online learning process. We use this term in our work because we need to take this evolution in our thinking about the online learning process one step further. Digitizing the learning experience is of little value if educators aren't first and foremost using digital tools to pursue significant pedagogical advancements. Some well-intended technophiles salivate over the latest innovation online, or on their smartphones, without focusing on the added effectiveness they intend to create. This is like handing a gardener a better shovel and focusing on the shovel rather than how it helps the gardener make the garden flourish. Focusing on that flourishing garden of using digital technology to enhance the online learning of K–12 students is the true intention of this book. To help flesh out what DEL is all about, let's address some essential observations about this concept.

Eliminate Physical Distance as a Barrier to Learning

Contrary to the old perceptions regarding distance learning, DEL is not just about overcoming the inability to meet face to face. In many cases, it is about the ability to make distance either irrelevant or at least less important to the learning process. It is about connecting students with previously unavailable learning opportunities, thoughtful instructors, dynamic resources, and engaging classmates in a platform of connectivity that produces a morphing cauldron of creative, new learning. It also creates more opportunities for classroom-based teachers and students to connect with each other outside of the classroom. To that end, the modern web-connected laptop has the power to bring learners the richest, most dynamic, and diverse learning experiences in human history.

Signal the Emergence of Learning- and Learner-Centered Facilitation

In a webinar, we invited Louisville, Kentucky, professor and pedagogy expert, Terrence M. Scott, to address an audience of teachers regarding approaches to creating highly engaging learning environments. During this live session, he presented several recommended classroom configurations designed to strategically maximize student engagement. Interestingly, each of his recommended configurations was designed to maximize learner-to-learner interaction and to try to create conditions where the teacher is the facilitator with learning at the center of what he or she does.

What we have found in a digital learning environment is that the platform itself serves to challenge the entire teacher-centric approach to education. Where traditional classrooms setups, with seats facing the instructor, are based on the premise of the class hinging on the facilitator's actions, modern-day learning platforms are constructed primarily around the content. Furthermore, although learning platforms aren't all the same, we have found that most of these learning platforms offer easy access for opportunities to dialogue with fellow classmates, encouraging connections.

Additionally, with powerful online platforms, educators can facilitate learning experiences by demanding much higher levels of learner engagement. These platforms and approaches to distance learning allow for greater degrees of personalization and opportunities for a teacher to intervene when the learner is struggling (Huang, Liang, Su, & Chen, 2012). They also allow for advanced levels of study once a student reaches basic competency. Using Khan Academy as an example, a mathematics teacher could provide virtual observations and interventions with a class full of students, each of them accessing different digital tutorials. While each student either seeks to reinforce learning by achieving prescribed competencies, or seeks advanced applications to promote even deeper learning, the teacher emerges as a facilitator for this process. As such, the teacher can use multiple tools to formatively assess students on a continuous basis to prescribe practice, resources, and other learning opportunities for students to meaningfully engage with content at their own pace and with earnest motivation to absorb the new learning. The mere fact that there are so many tools and opportunities available to diagnose learners and their needs makes DEL a must-use feature in traditional classrooms and gives it an advantage over traditional classrooms.

Provide Unlimited Learner Choice and Personalization

Giving learners a choice and opportunity to personalize their learning environment is an effective way to maintain student engagement. In many cases these choices or approaches to personalization come down to the student's preferred learning method and learning conditions (Spector 2013).

The learning method typically refers to the type of experience that stimulates student engagement in the learning. For example, a lesson that requires hands-on activities or is entirely visual has very different methodologies for instruction. For example, some methods might include the use of audio files or some type of simulation. Whenever possible, the choice in methodology allows learners to pick an approach that represents some unique novelty, perhaps in comparison to what they have been doing recently. The choice often represents a preferred way of processing information. Some learners for example, learn best by one or more of these approaches, or a blend of several at once.

Learning conditions refer to elements like the time of day, the length of engagement, and perhaps even details such as room temperature, body position, and so on. Many of you reading this book probably remember scheduling college classes and trying to pick learning opportunities that coincided with times of the day that met with your emotional and learning priorities. Indeed, some of us do like morning classes!

This discussion of methods and learning conditions is important because the allowances of technology provide learners the opportunity to put themselves in the situation where they can pick and choose their preferred learning method and condition. For example, a lesson may be posted in written form, with audio and video support, while simultaneously requiring some type of hands-on experience or experiment. In this case, the learner would engage in that activity and pick an approach that was most consistent with his or her preferred learning style. In terms of learning conditions, some students may find themselves logging in at the time of day when their energy is at its peak and can take breaks at a pace consistent with their personal levels of engagement. Clearly, allowing students to make these choices prepares them to be engaged with their own learning trajectory and capabilities.

To further illustrate this, we, your authors, use ourselves to reflect on the degree to which DEL provides each of us with options to personalize our own ongoing learning. Crystal Guiler is a digital native. When she seeks to learn something new, she first finds a blog on the topic and reads it to ascertain context. She then reads contributor feedback and may immediately post a question. After interacting in that space, she finds and listens to a posted lecture, followed by diving into the course readings, if applicable. Lisa Reason prefers to read the text first, then experience the noise of learner interaction on a discussion board or blog. Casey Reason would much rather listen to a lecture or debate, read the book, and then jump right in and participate in an asynchronous discussion.

Of course, there are many other routes a learner could choose on his or her way to digesting the content. Up until the era of DEL, K–12 learners had to largely rely on the dexterity of their instructor to provide learning opportunities commensurate with their natural, hardwired learning preferences. Think about how much more our students could learn if they could more seamlessly and strategically identify and make use of their learning preferences, thanks to the availability of varied digital learning opportunities.

In addition to giving learners more choice, DEL gives facilitators even greater opportunities to personalize the learning and individually prescribe activities for learners that allow for remediation and extra support as well as acceleration, if proficiency is already established. In a traditional classroom, the teacher is always playing "beat the clock," facilitating instruction and hoping an opportunity to personalize will manifest. Many DEL opportunities simply expand what's possible, minimizing the challenge of eroding time and maximizing the focus on finding the best set of activities and engagements for the learners who need them.

Offer the Advantage of Timeless, Asynchronous Learning

One of the loftiest aspirations we have for this book is to shine a huge spotlight on what we believe to be the underestimated and largely underutilized advantage of *asynchronous* (or *cyber-asynchronous*) *learning*, the ability to participate in the learning process at any given time. Tech advocates champion asynchronous learning as being transformational due to its convenience (Ge, 2012). However, the true gift of timeless, asynchronous learning is in the degree to which it aligns with the natural learning rhythms of human beings. With technology and strategically constructed asynchronous learning experiences, learners can participate and engage in learning and reflecting experiences in a much more flexible time frame, potentially leading to deeper learning and engagement (Koutsabasis, Stavrakis, Spyrou, & Darzentas, 2011). For example, a teacher could post a trigonometry problem online for the entire class and open it up to student debate in relation to possible approaches and resolution. In a brick-and-mortar, real-time class, a quieter and perhaps more contemplative learner may take longer to respond and, thus, not speak up at all. However, in an asynchronous learning environment, with additional time to reflect, his or her insights may be altogether different and his or her willingness to participate significantly enhanced.

In addition, given a digital, asynchronous learning opportunity, the learner is more likely to feel comfortable providing a thoughtful and measured response (Nandi, Hamilton, & Harland, 2012). This is because the student not only has more time to think about the discussion but also to look up information and resources to support his or her perspective. Virtual, asynchronous learning also levels the playing field in terms of participation. In an asynchronous learning space, learners emerge and contribute with no regard to gender, height, voice, ethnicity, or relative vivaciousness. Strategically facilitated, asynchronous learning creates a condition where the quality of one's ideas becomes the ultimate measuring stick.

Invisible geographical boundaries, increased learner engagement, personalization, and asynchronous learning—these are all significant benefits of DEL that we explore in this book. Of these, asynchronous learning deserves special attention before we dive into the deep end of the DEL pool.

Advantages of Asynchronous Learning

Think about how important ongoing dialogue and thoughtful verbal exchanges are to the learning process. Meaningful dialogue and dialogue-driven learning activities likely power your classroom. It powered you in college when you stayed up all night reflecting on newly formed adult values. Dialogue or communication in one form or another clearly informed Neanderthals as they scrambled to survive the northern latitudes during the cold phases of the Pleistocene Era, or the Ice Age. We are a species that works well when engaging in continuous conversation. It drives our innovations and stimulates natural learning rhythms. Technology, however, has provided us with asynchronous opportunities to communicate that may actually allow us to expand and improve this natural learning propensity.

The Ice Age notwithstanding, does a loud lecture in a room of twenty or two hundred students provide the optimal environment for communication and collaboration? Does sitting in an uncomfortable chair in a room with inconsistent sound levels and visual accessibility truly represent the most superior method of learning? How many times have you listened to a real-time lecture and wished you could ask the speaker to repeat him- or herself? In an asynchronous learning environment, each learner can play a recorded lecture back, read a classmate's statement several times to consider its meaning, and expand his or her view if the learner missed the message. These things aren't possible for students steering a classroom blackboard. Let us look at some advantages asynchronous learning offers students.

Asynchronous Learning and the Brain

Our brains require an indeterminate amount of time for a process called consolidation. Consolidation is literally the process of sorting out the utility or meaning behind any new learning experience (Harris, 2014; Steiner, 2009). After engaging in a science experiment, your brain releases the memory of the color of your teacher's tie because it's irrelevant. Your brain, however, *will* revisit and more deeply reflect on the frothy burst of energy you observed when you mixed calcium carbonate with hydrochloric acid.

This process of taking in new information and going through consolidation to sort out the meaningful from the meaningless doesn't happen for everyone in the same way or in the same time. Some of us need to observe the same phenomenon several times to help us to capture its importance and remember the correct elements of either the process or the outcome (de Jong, 2010).

Furthermore, what's also interesting about this process is that our brains rely on retrieval to bring forward memories or stored learning elements at times when that learning is relevant. Thus, students with varying speeds of retrieval power drive our classrooms. In traditional, synchronous classrooms, students who are fast retrievers tend to be rewarded. In teacher-centric learning environments, where the teacher moves from respondent to respondent very quickly, without the opportunity to explore answers in depth, will find that students who retrieve information quickly are oftentimes perceived as having superior learning power. Learning theorists have found that this ability to quickly retrieve is no demarcation of intelligence. In fact, slower retrieving students may be calling on a deeper and more comprehensive reservoir of stored, contextual learning before formulating a response (de Jong, 2010).

What does all of this mean for asynchronous digital learning? Asynchronous learning activities allow students to control content intake, listening and observing multiple times or rereading key elements for the sake of understanding. Furthermore, when dialoguing with one another in an asynchronous environment, students who are slow retrievers are given an opportunity to participate in a time frame that is comfortable for them (Magistro et al., 2015). Their reflections may be even deeper than some of their fast-retrieving counterparts and, as a result, their input may be richer and deeper (de Jong, 2010). Despite its digital visage, asynchronous online learning may allow us to learn and engage our brains in a far more natural and organic way than ever before (Harris, 2014; Steiner, 2009). As if these benefits are not enough, it also leads to more thoughtful communication.

Asynchronicity and Thoughtful Communication

One more often-ignored advantage of the asynchronous nature of the DEL environment revolves around the realization that every asynchronous comment hangs in virtual abeyance—waiting for random or directed consumption. This effect is different for an online classroom where there are consequences, than it is for people posting to some random website under anonymous pseudonyms. This is a powerful distinction because whatever documentation or commentary we provide in a digital learning environment must withstand the potential scrutiny of careful observation and analysis.

How many smooth-talking businesspeople and politicians struggle mightily when confronted with a word-for-word transcription of exactly what they said—unable to hide what might be a shallow or misguided message behind their velvet delivery or handsome visage? Learning in a digital environment requires participants to think more carefully about how they contribute, the words they choose, how to formulate their thoughts, and how to respond to others who do the same. If the words we speak face to face in real time were to hang in this virtual abeyance, we'd all probably be more careful about what we say and how we say it. Thus, asynchronous communication with DEL creates the right conditions for superior quality work.

This does not mean toxicity cannot creep in, of course. An important element related to the successful facilitation of distance learning revolves around the prevention and the appropriate response to toxic or inappropriate behaviors online. In an era when the challenges associated with cyberbullying and other attempts to threaten, dominate, and otherwise inhibit learning in a digital learning environment are rising, we will be focusing our attention on strategies that you can implement that will help you avoid these scenarios altogether by creating engaging learning experiences. Intervening when necessary is important; however, just as we have learned in the best examples of face-to-face pedagogy, the best way to avoid a classroom with off-task behaviors is to create an engaging learning environment where students are wrapped up in their work and don't have time to throw spitballs, cyber or otherwise.

Given online, asynchronous approaches' advantages, we believe the best modality for learning is one that strives to achieve balance or a blend between traditional (synchronous) and online (asynchronous) learning modalities.

Blended Asynchronicity

Blending both asynchronous and synchronous modalities gives students the opportunity to directly interact with the facilitator, ask questions, and develop a greater sense of connection to the facilitator, other students, and the content. The classroom's cyber-asynchronous components enable learners to work at their own pace, and eliminate time and work condition constraints that cyber-synchronous components demand (Ge, 2012).

Is it all exactly this simple? No. It never is. That is why we wrote this book, to give you a guide to facilitating learning online.

Goals for This Book

Technology has transformed more quickly than have our attitudes, assumptions, and instructional strategies. Many K–12 teachers still have very little experience with online learning or facilitating digital learning experiences. Furthermore, those who have begun to experiment with DEL, in many cases, do not feel entirely confident that the digital learning experience is as effective as they would like it to be (Li & Choi, 2014). This book is written with those educators in mind.

> ## HOW POPULAR IS ONLINE LEARNING?
>
> Five U.S. states (Alabama, Arkansas, Florida, Michigan, and Virginia) require K–12 learners to take at least one online class or learning experience or have the online learning experience incorporated into each course of the required curriculum, and North Carolina is testing such a requirement (Watson, Pape, Murin, Gemin, & Vashaw, 2014).

To better prepare these educators for the challenges and opportunities available in teaching online, we provide two things. First, we provide a philosophical overview in relationship to what is possible with DEL and how educators need to think about applying tools within the realm of technology to support online learning. Second, we provide direct guidance on the specific steps educators must take to set up, manage, and facilitate state-of-the-art online digital learning opportunities. To accomplish this, we address the following topics.

- Reflecting on the myriad of DEL applications available and the influences that shape our thinking about them

- Understanding the importance of a guaranteed and viable curriculum in designing, delivering, and assessing digital learning

- Understanding and applying best-practice strategies in setting up and initiating a digital learning experience

- Learning and applying practical strategies for designing engaging digital lessons and keeping the learners engaged throughout the learning experience

- Identifying best-practice recommendations in facilitating learner interactions and dealing with potentially disruptive or toxic learner interactions

In breaking down these topics into concise, manageable chunks, each chapter of this book establishes specific key questions that you will be able to answer upon completion of the chapter.

Finally, we hope this work provides a strong, philosophical framework to undergird the work of educators now and in the future—because we know that the landscape in digital learning will continue to change. We want this book to make you Monday-morning ready for these challenges and arm you with a mindset and philosophy that allow you to make good judgments as tectonic shifts in technology continue to occur.

To that end, throughout this book we offer educators a number of specific suggestions and examples related to pedagogical practices associated with digital learning.

However, to ensure the material is delivered in a succinct manner, we do not necessarily differentiate these illustrations and examples by various K–12 levels of application. This is purposeful. The knowledge you gain in this book will support your instructional practices involving digital learning at whatever level you teach. Digital learning modalities are simply tools that help you deliver your own best-practice-driven, grade-level or content-specific learning opportunities.

Therefore, this book is designed to assist you in your work to develop an online presence with your students that will extend learning well beyond the confines of a traditional classroom. If you work in a traditional setting, the suggestions in this book are designed to assist you in taking your class outside the bounds of time and space, and helping learners connect to subject matter in a more dynamic and meaningful way. If you are an online teacher, this book will assist you in creating more powerful, and personalized synchronous and asynchronous interactions that will assist learners to more dynamically connect with the content.

We hope this introduction challenges some paradigms and opens your eyes to the morphing possibilities in front of you. We designed this book to be more than just a theoretical intellectual exercise; it is also a guide to help you implement DEL in a consistent and effective way in your school. So let's break some paradigms, reframe, and get to work!

CHAPTER 1

Understanding the Modality and the Moment

There are a multitude of applications for online digital learning. This chapter is devoted to exploring some essential questions regarding the applications of this modality—this method for learning—and providing some observations that will help you put the learning in this book into the appropriate context. Let's start with some important questions about the modality of digital learning.

KEY QUESTIONS ANSWERED IN THIS CHAPTER

- What type of digital learning experience are you facilitating? How does it impact your approach?

- Who is planning and developing the online learning experience, and why does it matter?

- What opportunities do online tools offer, and what are the best methods for nurturing connectivity, learning growth, and innovation?

- How can technophiles and technophobes work together in facilitating online learning?

In thinking about these questions, consider the story of Nick, a fictional fourth grader at Eagle Cliffs Elementary School in Billings, Montana.

NICK AND THE SINS
OF SYNCHRONIZED LEARNING

Sitting neatly in a seat in a row with his books strewn at his feet and his notebook open, Nick worked diligently to take notes on the history lesson his teacher was providing. The notes on his page looked more like an Impressionist's painting than a well-crafted piece of prose. The edges of his papers were perpetually crumpled as his outstretched hands continued to manipulate, flatten, and perpetually rotate the paper to capture notes in some semblance of order. His head would bob up and down, trying to get closer to the paper and then pulling back. His feet nervously shuffled beneath him as looked up, down, and to the side for some inspiration as his frustration mounted. Nick was a kind and obedient boy, but he couldn't help noticing his classmates as they kept their words so neatly on the page.

One of Nick's greatest challenges in trying to keep up with his history lesson was the fact that all students were expected to work synchronously. Although the teacher presented the content as best she could, it was a long-standing expectation in her classroom that all the students would be able to follow all the content in a perfect synchronized moment, in the same exact way and at the same time. Nick couldn't do that, but that didn't mean the content was too much for him.

Learners like Nick may very well have the competency to engage this content with great depth and understanding, if they have the luxury of digesting the content at a slightly different pace or with slightly different support. Let's think about some solutions for Nick in a DEL environment that would help him meet his needs. Consider the following.

- The teacher might have presented the content in an audio or video format that Nick could access on his own device. This would allow Nick to pause it to reflect or take his time capturing the notes at his own pace. Or, he could go back and play a piece of the presentation again if he either didn't hear it or understand it. This is great for learners like Nick, or any of us that simply may have lost concentration for a moment.

- While taking the notes in a blended or fully online learning environment, Nick has several options. Certainly, the research on assistive technology shows us that students feel good about the fact that they can use the tools of technology to create written products that have a professional look. In this case, Nick wouldn't have to look to the left and right to compare his Impressionistic handwriting to his classmates. Instead, he would find that his writing is every bit as good and can be presented in the same form as everyone else.

- While listening to the presentation Nick can instant message a friend, or even his teacher, and ask for clarification or help. With fewer time constraints, he can wait for an answer. He also could quickly consult a myriad of resources that might help him understand.

- Nick could learn in his available setting and bring questions for clarification back to the classroom if videos and formative learning were offered online. This allows Nick a more personalized experience to his learning as he drives the learning with his specific needs in mind.

- Nick could learn fully online and have access to his teacher through the phone or Internet. This model allows him to collaborate asynchronously with other learners, provides the flexibility in time to manage his schedule, and allows him to join groups with similar interests to engage in socialization with peers.

As you have surely guessed, Nick is not the only learner who could benefit from DEL in this way. As you begin to consider how you can use DEL in your classroom, it's important to start with an understanding of the types of digital learning experiences available to you.

Types of Digital Learning Experiences

One complexity of embracing DEL is the variety of choices educators have for delivering digital learning opportunities to the learners they serve. Suffice it to say, there are some interesting choices that can significantly differentiate the experience. Consider the following questions.

- **Is your course or class asynchronous?** An asynchronous course is one in which learning experiences are shared without regard to the specific synchronicity of time, space, and events (Smith & Basham, 2014). This means that in your course you present learning opportunities that can be executed anywhere at any time. For example, the facilitator may post a mathematics problem in a digital course using an application such as VoiceThread. He may then ask learners to solve the problem, thoroughly explain their answers, thoughtfully debate, and reflect on each other's answers over the span of a week.

- **Is your digital class synchronous?** Sitting in a face-to-face college lecture or executing a typical K–12 lesson plan in a traditional classroom represents a synchronous learning experience. In other words, in a synchronous environment, all the learners experience the learning opportunity at the same time and in the same space. Therefore, a synchronous digital learning experience is one in which learning experiences happen in real time, and all participants engage in the learning experience simultaneously (Smith &

Basham, 2014). A teacher lecture or demonstration using Google Hangouts, Skype, or some type of webinar application represents an opportunity to provide a synchronous activity in a digital environment. Some K–12 digital schools have a student population who live hundreds or even thousands of miles away from one another, yet students' learning is almost entirely synchronous, with students logging on each day and greeting each other via Skype or Google Hangouts. Their learning is just as synchronous as the students you know who drive or walk to a brick-and-mortar building each day and pull up a chair beside their classmates.

- **Is your class or course an asynchronous-synchronous blend?** Some schools offer synchronous learning opportunities with face-to-face, real-time connections happening either in person or with the assistance of technology tools like Skype. Educators may then connect asynchronously by posting discussions or problems to be tackled by the class over a flexible, predetermined time frame. We've referred to blended learning multiple times already in this book. This type of class or course is an example of that.

  What's exciting about this option is that emerging evidence shows that this learning modality may, in some cases, provide learners with superior learning opportunities versus traditional, face-to-face-only instruction (Driscoll, Jicha, Hunt, Tichavsky, & Thompson, 2012). Our own experience supports these quantitative conclusions. Although there are K–12 learning experiences that are successfully facilitated in 100 percent asynchronous learning environments, we believe that the best approach is still a blended one in which there is at least some opportunity for synchronous contact and connection followed by asynchronous opportunities for learners to thoughtfully and meaningfully engage the instructor, their colleagues, and the content.

Believe it or not, you may already be teaching in a somewhat blended learning environment. Consider the following story involving a wildly popular, technophobic government teacher, Mr. Hill, and how he discovered he'd facilitated a blended learning environment without even realizing it.

DOUGLAS RETURNS THE FAVOR

Mr. Hill was a very successful government instructor at his local high school. Most of the students went on to college and had fond memories of their experiences with their charming and challenging senior-year teacher. An unapologetic technophobe, Mr. Hill always made the case—with great wit, volume, and exaggerated gesticulation—that technology and learning at a distance were leading to a cataclysmic erosion in creativity, brainpower, and the advancement of the human condition.

He was one of those rare teachers who could lecture consistently and hold the students in the palm of his hand. His stories were legendary, and his anecdotes were state-of-the-art cliff-hangers that kept students remarkably engaged. Unlike his teacher colleagues, he did not have a website and didn't post assignments or discussion notes online.

When a former student, Douglas, returned from college to visit Mr. Hill on the Friday before spring break, "the good Prof Hill," as Douglas called him, was delighted to see him. As a student, Douglas had been curious, thoughtful, and exceedingly well-read. While in high school, he was willing and able to engage Mr. Hill on a variety of topics, and their debates were legendary and thoughtfully humorous. Given their past penchant for debate, Mr. Hill seized on the fact that Douglas, now a student at a very prestigious Ivy League university, was taking one of his core classes online. With great volume and humorous gesticulation, Mr. Hill chided Douglas for his online learning, professing the inevitable downfall of civilization thanks to the crushing press of an overly digitized world. After taking a breath from his rant, Mr. Hill waited for Douglas to respond. With a small smile creeping on his face, Douglas simply said, "Your class is online already, my good Prof Hill."

For once, Mr. Hill was silent, then he smiled indignantly. "No, really, it is," Douglas continued. After gracefully popping open his laptop, Douglas took Mr. Hill on a virtual tour that the teacher would never forget. Mr. Hill's lecture notes, taken by his students, were posted and shared on Google Docs. Given Mr. Hill's popularity, numerous former students had compiled copious amounts of interactive feedback about his class content online. There was also a Facebook page dedicated to "Hillisms," with feedback and commentary from current students as well as those who had graduated a decade or more earlier. On a blog, students discussed course content, replete with scholarly references, YouTube links, and Snapchat rants to underscore their points. Douglas told Mr. Hill about the hours he had spent studying for his midterm and final, armed with group-text exchanges, instant-message-fueled cries for help from classmates, and a number of other seemingly endless digital connections reflecting on Mr. Hill's class.

Mr. Hill is an amazing teacher who engages his students and stimulates their curiosity and love for civics. Despite his attempt, however, to keep his learning environment synchronous, Mr. Hill's class had been summarily infiltrated by the technology tools of the day, adding asynchronous elements that undoubtedly enriched the learning experience for so many students. The brilliant Professor Hill always made Douglas think about things in new ways. On that day, Douglas returned the favor.

We share this story about Mr. Hill to reinforce the notion that, in many cases, asynchronous learning is already happening in our schools, whether we like it or not. It's almost impossible to deliver face-to-face content that isn't directly or indirectly assisted by tools that bring an asynchronous element to the learning process. This is important to note because technology isn't going away, and we're better off as a profession being strategic and purposeful about the tools at our disposal. Perhaps Mr. Hill could build on the asynchronous efforts going on around him and make his very good class even better. Of course, doing so will force him to carefully consider how to plan and develop his new online curriculum.

How to Plan and Develop an Online Curriculum

Developing an online curriculum that facilitates DEL requires you to think deeper about the nuts and bolts of your digital learning environment. The way in which the curriculum is presented makes a big difference in the degree to which the facilitator can personalize and tweak instruction to meet individual student needs. It also makes a difference in the way facilitators use and administer assignments and assessments in the course. Consider the following questions about curriculum and planning.

- **Did someone else already establish and write your digital learning curriculum?** If so, you are working with a curriculum that some other instructional designer from your area established. It may even come from an outside vendor who created a program that your school utilizes. In this case, your focus is on how to facilitate, further illuminate, and enhance what is already there.

- **Is the curriculum open shell?** With an *open shell* option, your school provides the course shell and the instructor engages in the planning, design, and delivery of instruction. Clearly this is a more challenging option. However, we also think that this is an option that drives the deepest level of innovation. Since the mid-2000s, many schools have successfully utilized prepackaged curricula; however, we believe that, as our culture becomes increasingly comfortable with digital learning options, schools will become more adroit at designing and delivering their own digital learning experiences. Without question, engaging in the design and development of digital learning experiences always enhances the process of working with colleagues to share ideas on planning and innovation strategies.

- **Who can join?** Most DEL platforms fall into one of two categories of membership: open or closed.
  - When membership is *open* for a digital learning experience, it includes learners who come together from a broad or potentially limitless geographic location (DuFour & Reason, 2016). A *massive open online*

course (often called a MOOC) is just one example of a type of digital learning experience that is available to anyone, with participants allowed to engage the learning in almost any way that meets their needs (Crow, 2013).

◆ A *closed* digital learning experience includes students from either a previously established learning group, such as an existing German 4 class that elects to work together online, or a recognized group of students who are assigned to a particular digital learning experience. Under this permutation, students may know one another before the learning experience, and the participants are derived from an organized grouping, such as from their local school or a charter school digital academy (DuFour & Reason, 2016). Most of the strategies in this book work most directly with this second, more common, K–12 closed digital learning option. Both options, however, have their place in online learning environments.

Given these differences, developing a curriculum that facilitates digital learning experiences represents a diverse set of challenges. Nuanced distinctions will emerge because of these different delivery formats and decision points, and we have constructed our recommendations in this book with these variances in mind. You will notice that we occasionally call out these differences and describe how facilitators may have to change their approach based on the differences in delivery we describe. However, for the most part, we assemble approaches that work in most of the aforementioned settings.

With this established, all the careful planning in the world may not mean much if the people using these online learning environments cannot work together with the provided tools.

Technophiles and Technophobes: Ending the Cage Match

Technophobes are those who fear and abhor the use of technology. *Technophiles*, on the other hand, wildly embrace it (Burnett, 2004). In your school, you may have noticed multiple collisions between technophiles and technophobes. These collisions happen in most any educational environment when it comes time to grapple with new opportunities to support student learning. Technophiles tend to seek every opportunity possible to digitize the learning experience, while technophobes fight them every inch of the way, claiming that valuable learning resources are lost if digital learning platforms take precedence.

We, the authors of this book, are certainly not technophobes. However, we do not consider ourselves uncompromising technophiles either. Our passion is learning. To that end, we do not believe technology is the answer to every question. We believe that solid, strategic, research-based pedagogy should be at the center of what we do and, whenever possible, we should utilize whatever implements are available to enhance that process. Thankfully, learning pedagogy has plenty of support from the emergence of numerous digital learning innovations (Amory, 2012). If we were to referee this cage match, we would tell the technophiles and technophobes that grappling over technology is fruitless and that a balanced approach will let them both turn their focus where it belongs—on learning.

Regardless of your outlook, technology has a clear and vital role to play in facilitating distance-based learning.

Program Options for Learning at a Distance

Although learning at a distance is growing in popularity, we must keep in mind that technology is not only changing the learning possibilities associated with facilitating experiences online but also program delivery options thanks to emergent technology, new, rapidly developing programs allow schools to reach learners and support their learning in unique ways, depending on their needs. Consider these eight institutional options in relation to the delivery of digital learning.

1. **Totally digital virtual schools:** In 2014, there were 135 full-time virtual charter schools in twenty-three states, enrolling over 180,000 students (National Alliance for Public Charter Schools, 2016). These schools are 100 percent virtual in their curriculum delivery.

2. **Charter schools:** With so many charter schools emerging with highly specialized, topical points of focus, there are obviously several occasions in which a distance learning option can be of great benefit. The National Alliance for Public Charter Schools (2016) estimates that in the United States there are as many as 6,400 charter schools in existence, several them offered all or in part online.

3. **Homeschooling:** There are more than 1.5 million homeschooled students in the United States (Snyder, de Brey, & Dillow, 2016). With the growing popularity of homeschooling, communities have established parental best-practice groups that work together to help ensure that parents provide competitive curriculum offerings for home-educated learners. Distance learning opportunities, which can represent all or part of curriculum delivery, increasingly fortify these home-based options.

4. **Alternative schools or credit recovery programs:** Since the 1960s, schools have attempted to come up with new and unique programs designed to help learners with alternative learning options and credit recovery (Raywid, 1999). These programs can be offered all or in part online. During the 2009–2010 school year, 88 percent of U.S. districts offered students credit recovery courses (Powell, Roberts, & Patrick, 2015). In New Hampshire, the Virtual Learning Academy Charter School offers sixty-two online competency-based credit recovery classes. Interestingly, research shows that online credit recovery programs often cost less than traditional programs and typically offer students a high degree of flexibility in that they can repeat classes at whatever time and pace meets their individual needs (Davis, 2015).

5. **Resolution to scheduling conflicts or curriculum supplements:** Many schools across the United States are investigating or using digital learning options as a mechanism for saving money on staffing and enriching their curriculum (Clark & Barbour, 2015). If, for example, a group of learners at a school is interested in the pursuit of fluency in a foreign language, it may be significantly cheaper, more efficient, and often more effective to join a virtual learning cohort where these options are available to learners without necessarily hiring a facilitator who must commit to living in the area.

6. **International connections:** Many emerging international digital schools offer a very interesting value proposition (Clark & Barbour, 2015). They provide a highly competitive, totally digital learning experience, which includes a steady diet of synchronous learning experiences (via Google Hangouts, as an example) that allow participants access to a highly rigorous curriculum, taught by an international cadre of teachers who bring unique expertise to the field. Furthermore, students in these international schools enjoy studying with classmates who come together from all over the world. These highly competitive digital learning environments are often appealing to students with an interest in the international business community because of the opportunity to establish international business connections at a very early age.

7. **Preparation for higher education and career training:** The number of college students who take at least one online course is increasing every year. For example, 26 percent of 2013 undergraduate students were enrolled in at least one online course, and that number grew to 28 percent in 2014. Thirty-three percent of graduate students were enrolled in at least one online class in 2014 (Kena, Hussar, McFarland, de Brey,

& Musu-Gillette, 2016). Therefore, preparing students for a more virtual orientation for future career preparation and training is important.

8. **Flipped schools with an asynchronous digital enhancement:** At their core, the digital learning phenomenon and the flipped school concept (where students view lectures at home and devote in-class time to discussions and activities) have both emerged with several interesting learning similarities. Both flipped schools and DEL platforms provide learners with control over how they access opportunities for direct instruction. In a flipped school, a middle-level science teacher may conduct an experiment, videotape it, and then post it online with some summative comments and perhaps a link to an additional resource for further study. Flipped schools follow this format to give learners who need more time an opportunity to reflect on what they're learning and to revisit key elements of the modality of direct instruction. This allows students to come to school and apply the learning with one-to-one, guide-on-the-side assistance from their teacher. This is the exact formula we use in most DEL experiences and it is one that teachers can use for their classrooms. This interesting, innovative similarity speaks to our evolution as a profession. Whether you're flipping your classroom or using DEL approaches in an almost totally virtual learning experience, we're keeping in context that it's all about the learning and finding strategic ways to bring students toward the desired learning goals. In the future, it's likely that many flipped classrooms will apply much of what we discuss in this book.

In reflecting on these different options, think about how wonderfully diverse each of these learning opportunities is from the others. Think about the types of students each opportunity likely serves. Technology gives us the ability to serve and support learners in a way that, before now, was just not possible.

Although this is just a part of what makes these such exciting times, you should also be mindful of the inevitable digital learning scams that complicate the online learning landscape.

Digital Learning Scams

We would be remiss if we did not speak to some of the unscrupulous vendors who take unseemly shortcuts en route to the allure of profiting from the scalability of digital learning environments. What these entrepreneurs have figured out is that digital learning offers unique scalability due to reduction in overhead. Let's assume that a state provides $10,000 per student for public, K–12 education. If the state has a voucher program and a family elects to take its $10,000 voucher and spend it on a school that delivers its education 100 percent online, an opportunity for unique profitability emerges. In this case, with the state allocation in hand, the absence of a brick-and-mortar schoolhouse to support the learning process creates remarkable savings. Delivering learning online also saves money on things like electric bills, custodial and support costs, sports programs, and so on.

In this kind of scenario for delivering online education, it would seem logical that the money saved could be reinvested in providing superior resources and potentially hiring state-of-the-art content facilitators. Sadly, this is often not the case. In fact, when it comes to instructors many of these for-profit seeking entrepreneurs hire poorly compensated adjuncts who ultimately work for a fraction per hour of their traditional K–12 counterparts—thus increasing an already robust bottom line (Desroches, 2016; Strauss, 2016). There have been several well-documented news stories over the years highlighting digital learning opportunities wherein students were placed in unusually large classes and taught by part-time instructors while collecting the full, state per-pupil allocation. Although these poorly conceived and poorly executed learning opportunities may look attractive to the economic bottom line, they hurt the cause of learning at a distance by sending the message that this modality is about profit. A quality digitally enhanced education makes this modality about advancing human potential, not profit.

How can you tell if an online learning entity is doing it right? Here are a few questions that will help you get at the truth.

- Does the school's goals or mission incorporate student focus?
- Does the school's strategic plan include personalized learning?
- Does the school hold relationships with quality organizations such as the International Association for K–12 Online Learning or Quality Matters?
- Is the school accredited? If so, what type of accreditation does it have, and how does that compare to other regional schools?
- What do employee comments on sites like Glassdoor (www.glassdoor.com) say about working conditions and administrative focus on students?

In addition to answering these questions, check to see if the instructors are full time or working in a largely adjunct capacity. For the most part we believe entities that commit full-time instructors to this work are more comprehensively engaged in supporting an appropriate model.

Also, try to determine the teacher salary range at that school. In some cases, less-than-admirable digital learning entities try to get away with paying faculty members a fraction of their potential salary in an equivalent face-to-face environment, attempting to trade convenience and flexible working conditions for salary. We, again, don't see this as a reasonable transaction. Working in your pajamas is a wonderful benefit, but it shouldn't be the driving force for saving money on high-quality instructors.

These are, unfortunatley, not the only issues you must consider when conducting your course online. Social media also has a big role to play.

Some Thoughts on Social Media

Despite its many benefits, social media has contributed to a great deal of bullying, unattributed ranting, predators, and countless scams and distractions. In some cases, it has probably contributed to the degradation of writing skills and critical thinking. Conversely, some of the most thoughtful educators we know utilize social media to enhance their instruction and as a mechanism for building resources and connecting with other innovative educators. We believe that social media will continue to evolve and will be a significant component in developing highly competitive digital environments. Tiffany Hallier, founder of OhSoSocial (https://ohso.social), is our social media specialist. She has given us insights into the evolving role social media plays with our work, including developing the following four guidelines for using social media to enhance education.

1. **All social spaces are not the same:** For example, with Twitter becoming perhaps the most preferred social tool for emerging news, if you are teaching a class that relies on current events, the inclusion of certain Twitter feeds might make your learning space more robust. Instagram, on the other hand, might be a less-than-ideal fit for this kind of class.

2. **All learning spaces are becoming social:** From how campaigns strategize for political elections to how corporate America markets its products, social media has an impact on everything in our culture. The same is true with learner management systems and almost any type of learning experience. If an educator in a digital environment or otherwise tries to make his or her learning antisocial, he or she is unlikely to be successful.

3. **Social spaces aren't forever:** Although our culture tends to enjoy the idea of permanence, social media connections don't have to go on forever. You can join a group on Facebook and then move on once the usefulness of that group expires. Having the ability to move on and look for other in-the-moment connections keeps social media interesting and allows for the greater prevalence of innovation.

4. **Schools need a strategy:** It is beyond the scope of this book to delve into too many details concerning social media, but we believe that social media is a very powerful tool if it is utilized strategically. Schools need to have a plan for their social presence. To make social media work, content needs to be consistently provided and thoughtfully scheduled for release. We believe this is true for large corporate and nonprofit entities, and it's also true for teachers who use social media with their students.

Use these guidelines as you consider how you might integrate social media platforms and tools into your own curriculum.

Conclusion

The introduction and this first chapter provide you with a much-needed philosophical backdrop for putting in context the strategies we will explore throughout the rest of this book. DEL doesn't represent a new direction or destiny in K–12 education. If executed appropriately, it instead represents an efficient, cost effective, and comparable, if not superior, learning opportunity for the students you serve.

Finally, in Zen practice, it's not uncommon to deliberately confront either the unfamiliar or irrational as an opportunity to extend the limits of one's intellect or understanding. Satirist Jon Stewart used to close his popular hit *The Daily Show* with a funny, obscure, or otherwise jarring image in relationship to the political thought of the day. Think of Mr. Hill, who had his moment of Zen when his well-schooled charge returned and gently confronted him with the jarring reality that his assumptions about technology and learning were wrong. In fact, his students could grow more with asynchronous elements dynamically providing all of the students the opportunity to think things through and respond. In a moment of Zen, Mr. Hill learned to embrace the opportunities provided. Mr. Hill never became a technophile, but that moment gave him the courage to inspire thoughtful consideration of the tools he had come to suddenly understand and even respect.

CHAPTER 2

Planning Curriculum, Assessment, and Preinstruction

Because many of you are in very different places in terms of curriculum expectations, we approach instructional planning in this chapter from a broad perspective that you can apply to your classroom's needs. As you conceptualize your curriculum, we attempt to clarify the methods of online teaching you can prepare as a precursor to launching your course. Here are some common questions that individuals ask when embarking on an online teaching endeavor.

KEY QUESTIONS ANSWERED IN THIS CHAPTER

- When choosing a curriculum program to plan and develop, what are its advantages and disadvantages?

- What are the implications of attention to appropriate instructional pacing?

- What are the implications of supporting learning content and skill proficiency?

- How do teacher teams inform the process of planning and developing online learning?

- What types of instructional activities work well online?

- What types of learning assessments work well online?

As you reflect on these questions, it's important to consider the degree of flexibility you have in constructing your online course's curriculum. Why is your flexibility as a facilitator a factor in implementing your online course? Consider the following conundrum that Dana faced in trying to implement beneficial change.

DANA AND THE INNOVATION STRANGLEHOLD

Dr. Reason,

I have been teaching for ten years and have the good fortune of coming from a school district that deeply embraced the Professional Learning Communities at Work model. I read the book you wrote with Dr. DuFour regarding virtual collaboration with great enthusiasm because of my recent career change (DuFour & Reason, 2016). I've always dreamed of being an innovative educator, and this fall I took a job with a national online middle school that serves at-risk students throughout the nation. They hired me because of my experience in working with PLCs and my background in supporting at-risk learners.

The teachers that I am working with didn't know much about the PLC process. During one of my first meetings, I had a chance to share with them the concept and talk about what steps we could take to begin to initiate the process. When I talked to them about defining, as a group, the essential learning our students needed to demonstrate, the group responded that the essential learning was already provided in the course platform. When I mentioned the importance of the establishment of common formative assessments, they again told me that the platform maintained these documents and no additional work in this area was needed. When I talked to them about making changes to the curriculum or our approaches due to discoveries that we might make along the way, my team again informed me that the curriculum was set and that we would have to go through the designated designer in order to make any changes to the curriculum.

Did I make a mistake by coming to this school? Are all schools delivering online learning this inflexible?

Help!

Dana

What you will discover in looking at what teachers are facing in teaching online is that there are numerous variables when it comes to designing a curriculum. In Dana's case, she clearly found herself with what she felt like was very little wiggle room in terms of design and delivery of learning thanks to joining this national, online delivery platform. We have seen other cases wherein teachers are asked to teach a high-stakes, relatively sophisticated class online and are provided little more than a cursory overview of what the e-learning platform can do and a good luck wish. This chapter is designed to help negotiate both ends of the continuum, as well as where most of us exist, which is somewhere in the middle.

Approaches to Curricula in Digital Environments

We have observed many prepackaged K–12 digital curriculum programs wherein, just like Dana, the instructors inherit a full complement of instructional units, individual lessons, and accompanying assessments when they log in to begin teaching. In Dana's case, she was in for a bit of a struggle in that the flexibility required for teachers to own their essential learning, their common form of assessments, their results, and their ability to adjust their work to continue to improve is indeed more difficult under this permutation. There are, however, curricula solutions that are not strictly prepackaged and offer instructors incredible freedom to design their courses. Both formats have inherent advantages and disadvantages, something we explore in this section.

Advantages of Prepackaged Learning

One advantage of a prepackaged curriculum, like the one Dana experienced, is its potential for offering teachers who are new to digital learning facilitation the opportunity to truly focus their attention on interacting with the students and optimizing the learning experiences. These curricula are not unlike a teacher in a traditional classroom receiving an outstanding lesson plan from a colleague. This said, it's important to establish that, although the heavy lifting has been done, these curricula still require excellence in execution.

Prepackaged curricula are also advantageous because, in many cases, the instructional designers have unique design approaches, access to content, and the ability to utilize the institution's support to procure some unique artifacts.

Let's revisit our friend Dana, who struggled mightily in wrapping her head around the inflexibility of the curriculum, assessments, and even opportunities for intervention and collaboration. The truth is she did experience some pleasant surprises. An avid scientist, Dana thought that she had some very impressive resources collected for her students. To her delight, she discovered that her digital school had invested in some exclusive content developed in support of the famous science superstar Bill Nye the Science Guy. His digital content was illuminating. This, combined with some additional hard-to-find resources from *National Geographic* and the Smithsonian Institution made Dana realize that, although the content was less flexible than she would have liked, the digital school had invested some meaningful resources in gaining access to some content artifacts that she never could have, either working alone or even with the best efforts of her local PLC.

A prepackaged, fully loaded, digital learning experience revolves around the ability to create immediate availability of a learning experience that a local school may be unable to provide. For example, if a student in Sheridan, Wyoming, wanted access to a level 5 Latin class, that school might be too small to offer such an advanced language. In these situations, the existence of a prepackaged curriculum may minimize the need for a specialized instructor who is available in Wyoming. It may allow an existing foreign language teacher, still a language expert, to teach a class that he or she may otherwise have a challenge preparing to teach.

Disadvantages of Prepackaged Learning

As alluded to in the example with Dana, there are significant shortcomings associated with utilizing prepackaged digital curricula. First, if teachers don't have the opportunity to actually participate in the construction of the curricula they use, they aren't as likely to fully embrace it. Second, teachers individually or collectively, miss out on opportunities to personalize the presentation of the curriculum. For example, if record snow falls in the winter, followed by dangerous flooding in the spring, had occurred in Wyoming, the teachers could use this real-time, natural occurrence to help teach some essential middle school science learning outcomes. With a prepackaged curriculum, the ability to appear responsive to the moment is sometimes diminished or lost.

Another disadvantage is a loss of autonomy in establishing quality forms of assessments. Although a benchmark assessment can tell teachers a great deal about their progress with their students, quality formative assessments allow teachers to quickly ascertain how their students are doing and adjust their approach accordingly. Indeed, without this flexibility there is a significant chance that the curriculum will be taught without consideration to if students are learning it or not.

Furthermore, prepackaged online learning curricula often do not include district or building learning objectives. K–12 education often attempts to establish curricula uniformity, in terms of collective expectations for teaching and learning, that prepackaged curricula may fail to take into consideration. This is often the case if the curricula are developed outside that district or building.

Open Shell Instructional Design

Open shell curricula are the counterbalance to prepackaged ones. With this model, the school provides teachers with a learning management system (LMS; see chapter 3, page 42) and an open shell course that has the capacity to host several virtual learning opportunities for the instructor to plan, design, and deliver. Under this permutation, teachers must figure out how to take what might be existing content and learning expectations and create digital learning experiences that can be uploaded onto the LMS assigned to them. Perhaps the most simplistic way to illustrate what this is like for someone who isn't familiar with learning at a distance is to imagine logging into Facebook for the first time, putting in your email and password to get started. Although it is at a more simplistic level, joining Facebook provides you with an open shell wherein you have to construct the artifacts and upload the pictures to make your space come alive.

This modality's primary advantage is that it allows teachers to create their content and personalize their approach pursuant to the students they serve and their own expertise. This approach does, however, put a greater burden on teachers as facilitators. If facilitators have little or no practice in developing learning experiences online, their courses may not be as well crafted as researched, prepackaged curricula offerings. Certainly, with many years of experience, well-seasoned outside curricula designers can oftentimes save the district time and, at the very least, provide a great head start in terms of establishing what some of the possibilities for digital teaching and learning might look like.

Consider that, before she was hired in her new position, Dana had experimented with offering online content with her students. She found a free, open shell platform, called Moodle, for her work. In navigating this open shell environment, she found she had access points that allowed her to load students into her classroom, and upload content, videos, ebooks, and other teaching artifacts. She also had a simple quiz maker and some tools that allowed her to organize her students into groups and give them access to other students outside the classroom. This was very beneficial to her as a teacher, but it was not without its challenges. When she received her administrative privileges for the platform, she had to do quite a bit of learning to navigate this open shell environment. It was extensively empty until she filled it up with dynamic learning opportunities.

Instructional Activities and Approaches

Although we believe that, all things being equal, the learning process is enhanced when teachers have greater degrees of control, teaching in a digital environment is unique, and creating content that's meaningful and engaging takes some time and practice. When you're just starting out, especially if you're working within the guidelines and framework that your school district has set up, there can be a huge benefit to starting with prepackaged digital curricula that myriad outside experts had a hand in designing. Don't assume that these packages don't have the capacity to meet the unique standards of your district or students.

In a perfect world, schools could provide teachers with access to prepackaged resources designed for online learning that allow for flexibility and local adaptation. This is not unlike the resources we use from publishers who provide us with quality materials in conjunction with textbook adoption. Due to the unique nature of learning online, it's helpful to experiment with prepackaged curricula. With that said, it's critical to make your choices with an eye toward the future. There is no question that this modality of instruction will continue to grow in the years to come. Even if developing your own online curriculum from scratch induces some growing pains, getting started in developing those professional competencies in your school district puts you in a great position to continue to grow as the technology improves, the demand escalates, and the profession continues to evolve.

In this chapter, and moving forward in this text, we want to provide you with some ideas on specific activities that work quite well in a digital environment. Irrespective of the digital platform you use to engage students in DEL, it's critical that you engage in this learning experience with all of your creative energies at your disposal. To that end, let's look at some best-practice approaches to content delivery that facilitators of DEL may elect to use to meet and exceed key academic standards.

Content Demonstration

DEL facilitators can conduct a demonstration, such as a science experiment or a thoughtfully articulated lecture, either synchronously in front of a live streaming video camera or asynchronously in the form of a digital recording. In instances when instructors work with students synchronously online, they may elect to record that experience for students who are absent or for those who will benefit from reviewing it to obtain a more comprehensive understanding. There are also third-party sources with ready-made recordings that you can incorporate into your curriculum. One of the more popular tools for facilitating this kind of content demonstration comes from Khan Academy (www.khanacademy.org). Khan Academy offers a number of well-explained content demonstrations that teachers can use, either as part of a synchronized learning experience or asynchronously in the form of a posted lesson, for students to review or dig even deeper for advanced learning opportunities.

We predict that in the future most teachers will make a great deal of use of digital captures of key content artifacts, whether they're working in the online learning environment or a traditional one. Having key content demonstrations saved as supporting artifacts helps support learning for students who miss a lecture, need more time to review, and so on.

Group Work and Team Projects

Virtual learning environments are an ideal space for group work and team projects. Although groups can connect with one another synchronously with tools like Google Hangouts, actually hearing each other's voices and seeing each other's faces in asynchronous communication via VoiceThread, Present.me, Prezi, Audacity, Google Docs, Dropbox, or some other digital presentation and document-sharing platform puts learners in a position where they must thoughtfully communicate with their teammates in planning and executing team project assignments. This can be remarkably advantageous because, in the context of group work where distance separates group members, the opportunity to access resources and connect even more with the outside world could drive the group's work to even greater levels.

Virtual Field Trips

Dwindling budgets, tight schedules, and other logistical difficulties make conventional field trips difficult to execute. However, exploring the world at a distance using some unique tools gives facilitators the opportunity to share with students learning experiences from across the globe. Learners can explore the Arctic (ecology, geography, and science) through Polar Husky (www.polarhusky.com). With Global Trek (http://teacher.scholastic.com/activities/globaltrek), students can keep a digital journal to record what they learn from their virtual trip and acquire information about various countries. Students can explore the Louvre (www.louvre.fr/en/visites-en-ligne). And NASA offers virtual field trips (www.nasa.gov/dln/field-trip). (**Visit go.SolutionTree .com/technology** to access live links to the websites mentioned in this book.) There are plenty of other field trip options you can use to inspire learning related to your instruction and expand the world for students. Simply search for *virtual tours* or *virtual field trips* to find a plethora of offerings.

Games and Simulations

The gaming world has undeniably changed how we learn. Games and simulations are increasingly utilized in the military and in other venues as mechanisms for stimulating engagement, making learning fun, and giving learners an opportunity to apply what they know (Kapp, 2012). We have worked with leaders in the gamification industry and have seen how gamification can improve learning. As gaming continues to evolve, we recognize that facilitators will become increasingly creative in bringing games and simulations into their courses. Without question, more tools will evolve and facilitators of digital learning experiences will have a chance to enjoy and apply these solutions. For example, Jane McGonigal developed a game called EVOKE: A Crash Course in Changing the World. During the course of ten weeks, participants of the game receive an *urgent problem* and are then asked to read the story behind the problem, investigate the story, and then accept and pursue a mission to discuss and offer a solution. As participants complete objectives, they earn credits toward winning the game. Within the scope of the game, participants come up with creative solutions to our most pressing world problems: hunger, disease, water supply issues, climate change, and so on.

McGonigal also developed a game called SuperBetter to help individuals build resilience, motivation, and optimism. Essentially, participants receive a daily quest to adopt a new talent, habit, or improve a skill. Once they complete the quest they earn a badge and then move on to the next level of the game. Instructors can create badges through sites such as Credly (www.credly.com) or Open Badges (www.openbadges .org). In the very near future, you will find a growing selection of games offered through various online resources that will help you facilitate high levels of learning in the classroom. In the meantime, you can build more simplistic versions of games through the creation of projects in the classroom that require high levels of thought and interaction among learners.

Real-World Applications

Another advantage of learning at a distance is the capacity to make direct and meaningful connections with the outside world. Although there are certainly a number of concerns with sending students off to interact with individuals outside of the school setting, blogs and other virtual learning platforms provide students with connections to the outside world that can expand and enhance their understanding of, and ability to apply, concepts and skills in a practical and dynamic manner. For example, many safe online blogs, such as *Edmodo* (www.edmodo.com), provide students with opportunities to participate in service learning for real-world applications of learning experiences. These blogs offer contained, instructor-supervised environments that give the instructor administrative rights to delete and monitor all communication. Another valuable resource is Character's service learning page (http://character.org/key-topics /service-learning), which offers hundreds of lesson plans across a range of subjects and levels in an effort to support service learning in the classroom.

Open-Source Projects With Partners Everywhere

You may already know the term *open source* as something typically applied to free use of software applications. It actually has much broader implications, including for DEL. Online learning gives facilitators an opportunity to use an open-source strategy to facilitate learning connections with individuals who can provide valuable insights and information that make the learning experience real and meaningful (Li, 2010; Tu, Sujo-Montes, Yen, Chan, & Blocher, 2012). For example, you might put students into groups and require that each group come up with a viable solution to a real-life problem, such as a regional water safety issue. You may then send the learners out on the web in search of answers from chemists at various region and state water departments. You might encourage your students to find contact information and email chemists to find the best solution to the problem. They might also set up a blog and invite others to share opinions and solutions in order to construct a viable solution. Facilitators could ask student groups to present their solutions to the other groups, via either written word or podcast, and invite those groups to provide input into the viability of their solution and offer suggestions for improving and revising their proposed plan. In this way, students learn how to use the intellectual capital of others to build on their own ability to solve problems.

Activity Optimization

As you look over this list of activities that work well in a DEL environment, it's easy to see that each activity requires a unique level of individual learner engagement. It's important to match the activity to the learning outcomes you seek. For example, if you are working online for the first time and trying to teach a unit on photosynthesis, you should choose an activity that allows you to observe your students' work so you can detect whether they are fully engaged and participating in the lesson.

Many learning management systems allow you to track whether or not students watched the video all the way through, took a digital quiz, or engaged in a digital conversation. In many cases, you can track just how long students spent working online. Having worked with educators over the years to develop curricula that work in the online space, we have found that in most cases teachers find that their most creative lessons translate quite well from the physical world to the digital. Now, let's have a look at your assessment options in this environment and how the tools at your disposal might be more plentiful than you previously imagined.

Assessment in Online Learning Spaces

Almost everything in an online classroom can be tracked and recorded. This gives assessments delivered via digital learning platforms a big advantage over assessment in a physical classroom. Within a digital classroom, we can gather data about everything that is said and done, and therefore can gain a more dynamic perspective of student learning growth, struggles, and needs.

In this section, we provide an overview of some broadly positioned DEL strategies that will undoubtedly be helpful for enhancing your assessment when working with this modality. Many of these strategies are familiar to traditional K–12 instructors; however, there are some unique advantages in using these strategies in DEL environments.

- **Multiple-choice questions:** An advantage of most of the available DEL platforms is the capacity to create multiple-choice or true-or-false quizzes that can immediately provide the learner with feedback on his or her answers (see figure 2.1). In many cases, a facilitator can program a multiple-choice-quiz maker to quickly tell the student whether he or she answered the question correctly and then explain why the preferred answer is indeed the best. This strategy provides the instructor with quick, formative assessment information that doubles as a useful learning tool for students to reflect on their answers.

Stem: In the following, solve for x in $3x + 2 = 20$.

   a. $x = 20/3$ (Incorrect answer. Feedback: You made a good attempt, but don't forget to subtract 2 from both sides of the equation as a first step to solve.)

   b. $x = 54$ (Incorrect answer. Feedback: You made a good attempt. Remember to divide both sides of the equation by 3 after subtracting the constant from both sides of the equation.)

   c. $x = 6$ (Correct answer. Feedback: Great work! You have thought very hard about this problem and subtracted the 2 from both sides of the equation before dividing both sides by 3.)

   d. $x = 18$ (Incorrect answer. Feedback: You made a good attempt. Remember to divide by the x coefficient after subtracting the constant from both sides of the equation.)

Figure 2.1: Example of immediate feedback from a DEL algebra course.

- **Short-answer quizzes or tests:** Depending on the method and platform of content submission, in many cases the instructor is able to read the short-answer essays and then respond, creating a direct dialogue between the facilitator and the student. The facilitator is also often able to make visible changes to the student's answer to offer guidance. This allows for far more open dialogue that can make pursuing answers to those short-answer questions more meaningful.

- **Student presentations:** The first advantage in a student presentation in a virtual learning environment is that it can very easily be recorded and observed again. This allows us to double-check the presentation for accuracy and any other missing elements. The teacher can also give students the opportunity to post their presentation utilizing some sort of virtual projection software that allows students to rehearse their work and put their best foot forward. Furthermore, being able to post these recorded presentations guarantees that other students can observe their classmates; part of the assignment could direct students to provide commentary regarding their observations. Certainly, presentations like these can be submitted in a traditional classroom under these same permutations; however, in digital learning spaces this is an altogether common phenomenon.

- **Student-performance observations with immediate feedback (one to one or group):** With synchronous technology and the ubiquity of digital cameras, facilitators can make very careful observations of students as they engage in proficiency demonstrations pursuant to assigned tasks, such as individual assignments, group assignments, or formative assessments. A science teacher, for example, might be able to learn a lot about her students' knowledge regarding a dissection assignment by asking the students to perform the activity in real time while utilizing a digital camera to capture their work as they proceed through a required set of steps. In what previously would have been a dissection wherein it might have been very difficult for a teacher to see what individual students in a class of twenty-five are doing, the power of the camera and the convenience of handheld devices allow teachers to be right on top of the learning, reinforcing student progress each step of the way.

- **Essay and extended-response reflections:** Because online tools make it so much easier to make comments in a student paper, point directly to specific elements of the project, and even make explicit commentary, students can retrieve much more information from their instructor than ever before. The technology exists for facilitators to provide audio clips as commentary throughout the learning experience. Finally, because DEL environments are replete with so many opportunities to dialogue and connect, DEL facilitators have an opportunity to utilize the grading process in essays and extended-response assessments as an opportunity to maintain an ongoing dialogue with the learner about his or her learning experience. Just as an ongoing dialogue with a colleague fluctuates between text message, email, and phone or Skype modalities, the feedback provided with highlighted, trackable comments in a paper can evolve into yet another ongoing opportunity to engage the learner and keep the conversation moving in a powerful and purposeful direction. Figure 2.2 shows an example of this in action. Note that the highlighted feedback from the teacher would appear in blue on a screen.

As a result of the relationship between the two characters, three children were born to do amazing things. First of all, this is a great sentence leading to the discussion of the father's impact on his children and how each of them took a part of him with them. How can you articulate this without the word *amazing*? Are there other words you can use, or could you expand on the statement that they are amazing by explaining how the chosen professions are amazing? The first child grew to be a healer, the second grew to become a holy man, and the third child grew to be a teacher. Each served a part of the father's personality and made the family proud. This is a good connection to make and represents the writer's intended meaning. There is a great video from the author himself. Visit www.author.com/?ctlmtr to see it. I would enjoy hearing your thoughts!

Figure 2.2: Essay feedback with track changes.

- **Breadcrumb evidence for formative assessment:** Good instructors have always known that it is imperative they consistently assess their students' progress. Ongoing assessment provides an opportunity to adjust instruction and to consistently help each student meet proficiency expectations. One of the unique advantages of working in either a blended or completely digital learning environment is that most of the teacher and student interaction that takes place in written format is captured and hangs in digital abeyance. What we mean by this is that in many cases a teacher will provide some sort of written feedback for the work, and that form of inquiry, or even reteaching or support, is presented in a way that a student can go back and read again. Rather than simply making a verbal correction for a student who may not understand the content, an ongoing written commentary creates a breadcrumb trail that both students and instructors alike can follow en route to better ascertaining just how close the student is to reaching proficiency.

- **Organization and access:** Another advantage that DEL offers in relationship to managing and facilitating the learning experience goes back to organization and access to materials. When a facilitator in a face-to-face learning experience hands out a rubric, he or she must hold his or her breath and hope that the students don't lose that key resource when it comes time to execute the assignment. In virtual learning spaces, resources can be posted. If a student prints out and loses or accidentally deletes one of those resources, he or she can obtain a duplicate copy online. Furthermore, most virtual learning spaces allow students to maintain organized folders for their work. This can evolve into a portfolio of learning experiences that helps students stay organized and look back at their progress. In the face-to-face world, there are always K–12 students whose work suffers from poor organization and lack of relative neatness. In a virtual learning experience, students' ability to visualize and apply these tools may, in many cases, help them improve their organization and capacity to learn.

In 2015, Casey worked with a doctoral student, whom we'll refer to as Charles, who was interested in doing a dissertation related to DEL. Specifically, this student wanted to pursue a topic related to assessing learning in digital spaces. He was especially interested in the topic of cheating. The following is a paraphrased retelling of that conversation.

CHARLES AND THE REJECTED THESIS

Charles: Dr. Reason, as directed, I have been working over the past several weeks on some ideas regarding a dissertation topic. I think I'd like to write a dissertation on assessment in online learning spaces. Specifically, I am interested in the whole topic of cheating. It is my observation that cheating in digital learning is way out of hand. Many of the papers you have read over the years delivered digitally were probably written by somebody else. I think we need to do some research in K–12 and to see the impact of this cheating on assessment.

Dr. Reason: Charles, that sounds like an interesting topic. The issue of cheating does impact our ability to assess. How do you see cheating online as being more of an issue in a digital learning space versus a more traditional learning environment?

Charles: Well, the work is done online. Students could find papers from virtually anywhere and turn them in.

Dr. Reason: Charles, other than a blue book assignment, where a professor would stand over you and watch you compose your answer, hasn't the possibility of finding someone else to do you work, or cheating it as you have described it, always existed? Furthermore, I would suggest that the case can be made that it is much more difficult to cheat today than it was before. Today, I can take every piece of prose that is sent to me and run it through a myriad of content scanners that allow me to evaluate whether this is content that has ever been published elsewhere. It would seem to me that cheating is more difficult today than ever.

Charles: Wow. That makes sense. By the way, what's a blue book?

We share this brief story with you because assessment in digital learning spaces has some unique advantages that traditional teachers who never worked in the space may not be aware of.

Conclusion

This chapter provided you with a thorough look at the multiple options at your disposal in establishing your curriculum and creating elements for a system of ongoing assessment. As we have stated, we think that there are many advantages in developing and delivering curriculum in an online learning environment, from establishing useful instructional activities and assessments to working seamlessly with other teachers and a team, examining the breadcrumbs and evaluating your progress. Now that your content is ready, let's prepare to teach an online course!

CHAPTER 3

Preparing the Learning Experience

I n this chapter, we examine the steps K–12 facilitators must take to prepare to launch a quality online learning experience. We address how best-practice facilitators set up their online classrooms in a manner consistent with the ideals we've discussed so far. This includes learning about and choosing an LMS and organizing the student learning experience to produce effective outcomes.

KEY QUESTIONS ANSWERED IN THIS CHAPTER

- How do you organize the online classroom to encourage engagement and minimize frustration?

- What strategies can you employ to help learners feel comfortable, committed, and motivated to engage in the course?

- How do you set up structures for communication that allow for clear, professional, and dynamic interactions?

- How do you communicate and provide necessary support for learner performance expectations?

- What strategies are available to support diverse learners and those with special needs?

To answer these key questions, it is useful to understand the platforms and technologies that make learning online viable and efficient.

Learning Management Systems

We briefly touched on the concept of the learning management system in chapter 2. At its most basic level, the LMS serves as the host for an online learning experience. An LMS is a platform that supports the monitoring and delivery of subject matter to learners. Essentially, these systems provide facilitators with a platform to present information, communicate and interact with learners, and track their growth and progress (Lee & Lee, 2008).

Depending on the system your school implements, an LMS can be elaborate and costly, while others are open source (free) and incredibly straightforward to use. The platforms' scope and capabilities grow with each passing day. For this discussion, we do not delve into the intricacies of how an LMS works and its various hosting capacities. Suffice it to say, when a school or district considers an LMS, they should know there are a variety of options, and they must first and foremost make sure that data shared in this platform, including information about students and their families, are secure. In this section we examine how to evaluate LMS features as well as what qualities make for an exemplarly LMS.

Evaluation of Learning Management Systems

From a learning standpoint, we like to evaluate the LMS based on its technical features pursuant to the goals and objectives of DEL. Your LMS should not break down and should allow easy access to all the various working spaces within. Additionally, the LMS should be intuitive and easy to use. Contrary to distance learning in the early 2000s, most contemporary systems are designed in such a way that tutorials are rarely needed. Instead, users can often simply log in and figure things out for themselves, not unlike using a social media platform such as Facebook. Although the true workings of an LMS include many technical attributes, the best way to evaluate the system is to view the home page. Figure 3.1 illustrates an example of the home page for a relatively intuitive LMS. Notice how quickly your eye is led to the major elements of the course and the accessibility of the learning experience.

Although we attempt to provide you with ideal scenarios for establishing a well-organized LMS throughout this chapter, many of you will inherit a system from your school or district and may have very little opportunity to provide input regarding LMS choice or the organization of its elements. Keep in mind, however, that even if the LMS you are working with lacks the well-appointed accoutrements described here, much of the course's effectiveness relies on your facilitation and deployment of the best practices we recommend throughout this book.

Exemplars of Learning Management Systems

As you no doubt realize, technology is consistently improving in terms of its scope and capacity while simultaneously coming down in price. This access

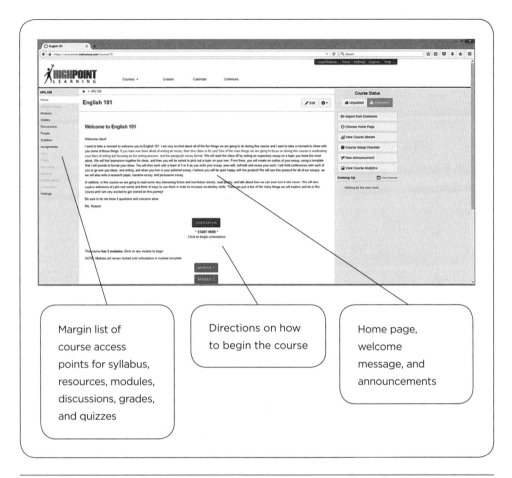

Figure 3.1: Example of an LMS course home page.

and affordability makes LMS adoptions easier. We think these free, and increasingly serviceable LMSs will continue to emerge and offer schools a competitive option to pay-for services. Moodle (www.moodle.org), for example, is shareware. This means a myriad of interested techies from all over the world had a hand in constructing this system in hopes of developing a superior product that is also free for anyone to use.

Although free is good, there are merits to looking at some innovative pay-for LMS platforms that are shaping the work of teaching and learning online. For example, Terry Nelson is the CEO of an LMS provider called Fishtree (www.fishtree.com). He actually cringes when we refer to Fishtree as an LMS. Yes, Fishtree executes all LMS functions such as hosting content, allowing educators to upload resources, and the like. However, this platform is designed to consistently scan posted curricula and evaluate them against proposed content standards or proficiency expectations. While a teacher is posting a lesson on Newton's first law, for example, a sidebar scans and posts required learning expectations or proficiency standards so that the teacher can make sure that her work is aligned.

Furthermore, in constructing and updating its LMS, Fishtreemaintains three priorities: (1) An LMS must be ready to be mobile and to work on mobile devices; (2) it must work with an awareness of all things social, meaning it must be able to stay connected to social learning tools like Twitter and Facebook; and (3) it must be adaptive, allowing teachers to be creative in developing and adapting their content. These priorities are interesting because they help us see how hosting and launching a curriculum can impact how it is experienced.

Most LMSs aren't as comprehensive as this. However, we believe that in the future these tools will continue to evolve and they will not only host our content but help us to find new resources and even push us toward more creative options in serving our students.

In a traditional classroom, the organization of the seating chart, the establishment of learning centers, and other logistical accoutrements make a significant difference in the learning experience. With DEL, the organization of your LMS is also a conduit to that success.

Organization and the Learning Experience

Research suggests that organization is essential to the online course experience for both facilitators and learners (Wright, 2014). If a course room is too difficult to navigate, students may experience cognitive overload and shut down. Therefore, all elements in the course room need to be clearly labeled and easy to access. In other words, when we organize information in an easy-to-access manner, we reduce one's memory load, making it easier for him or her to engage in what matters most (Cowan, 2014). Logging into a well-organized classroom that shows evidence of thoughtful preplanning makes a significant, positive impression on the learner.

Because organization is critical to learner outcomes, it is extremely important to give yourself the time to set up and organize your virtual learning classroom (Quinlan, 2011). This is especially important if you are new to this process. Ideally, the technical administrators who load the course allow you a week or more in the classroom to set up the learning experience and ensure that all of the working elements are in place.

There are nine essential steps involved in setting up your classroom and preparing your space for high-quality student learning, which we outline in the following sections.

Introduce Yourself by Posting Your Biography

In most LMS platforms, there is a place reserved to post an introduction. During course setup, it is important for you to introduce yourself by posting your biography.

When it comes to writing your bio, you have some latitude as there are many well-formed biographies out there with a large degree of variation. We recommend that instructors include a friendly and professional picture, if the technology allows. Depending on the students' age, varying degrees of formality are required when choosing a picture. In some cases, a slightly more casual, but still friendly and professional picture may create an even more inviting introduction to the course. In other cases, the students may already know you.

Even if you are familiar to the learners, we still suggest that you post a bio and include a friendly and professional picture. When students log in and see your picture, they will associate every correspondence they have from that point forward with that picture. Human beings respond well to visual images, and stimulating learning requires a human connection. Sharing yourself in this context is essential because research clearly shows that creating the correct foundation for the course is vital in facilitating a successful online course in which teaching presence, cognitive presence, and social presence may grow (Wright, 2014).

We recommend sharing a brief synopsis of your professional background, experience, and training, with a description of an outside hobby or interest you pursue. A brief mention of your family is nice as well. Keep in mind, however, that this is not the space to divulge deeply personal pieces of information with your students, and their interest in the personal details of your life is limited. They need to see that you are human, but they do not need to know everything about you. Figure 3.2 provides an example of a facilitator bio.

Hello Class,

I am Ms. Smith, and I will be your course facilitator for your ninth-grade English class. I have been teaching English classes for twenty-two years! I enjoy teaching writing skills and particularly like helping students with the writing process. I find that by going through every step of the writing process, students produce much better work. I am a mother of twin fourteen-year-old boys, who, like you, are in the ninth grade. I also like to hike and travel in my free time. Never forget that I'm here to support you, so please don't hesitate to reach out to me with anything I can help you with as we move forward with this class. I look forward to working and learning with you!

Figure 3.2: Sample facilitator bio.

Did you notice the enthusiasm expressed in the language and the judicious use of exclamation points? Enthusiastic words and a closing exclamation point make a big difference, because they show that you are engaged and excited about the new learning. Research clearly shows that when teachers are viewed as being enthusiastic about the learning experience, students are more likely to engage at a high level (Visser-Wijnveen, Stes, & Van Petegem, 2014). Furthermore, she was very deliberate about telling her class that she was there for them and looking forward to supporting them.

In face-to-face encounters, you may find that your students sense your sincerity and friendly facial expressions thanks to eye contact. In a digital learning environment this is more difficult to organically attain. As a result, we have to use tools of language, and even something as benign as punctuation, to help communicate our emotional intentionality and commitment. But make no mistake, words matter. How many times have you received a short text from a friend or family member and recognized that something was amiss? Put another way, don't most people you know write messages to you in a voice that you're familiar with? Unfriendly people tend to write short, terse messages that illuminate their sense of self-absorption. Conversely, the people you care about send messages that reinforce that intention. Your job in making DEL work for you is to make sure that you pay attention to the linguistic details and send messages that communicate your intentions.

Identify Resources to Enhance Instruction

It is important to identify resources—such as articles, tweets, expert pages and websites, videos, audio files, and so on—that will enhance instruction and to set up the course so that these resources are readily available to the students. The following are some guidelines to keep in mind.

Present a Variety of Resource Archetypes

In today's technology-rich world, learners enjoy accessing information in a variety of ways depending on their learning style and preferences. For example, some learners are happy to first explore a reading, reflect on a blog or synthesis of subject matter, and then listen to a video or audio discussion of the subject matter. Others will first run to Wikipedia to establish a baseline definition, look for a video explanation from YouTube (preferably less than three minutes in length), and then go in and read the written content. We think this process variability is extraordinarily beneficial in that everyone has a different learning style that may make one pathway or another more intuitive for comprehending the content. In most traditional classrooms the resource is the teacher and his or her accessibility or delivery may or may not be most effective for the learner. Therefore, we encourage teachers and teams of instructional designers to fortify the learning experiences with various content archetypes so that learners can make choices that make sense to them.

Encourage Learners to Go Out and Play

Although the student's age, sophistication, and degree of web filtration may have an impact in available learning resources, whenever possible, it is extraordinarily beneficial to encourage learners to find their own resources and to bring those resources to the conversation. This could include having students seek and contribute contrarian perspectives and alternative points of view. In our own training spaces, primarily driven by adult use, we have found that many will find new and incredibly beneficial resources that add to the training experience for everyone involved.

Know Your Sources

As the euphoria and excitement washes over us as we realize the seemingly infinite number of information sources available at our fingertips, we are reminded that not all sources are created equal. Sadly, the information age finds itself struggling mightily with a click-counting, digital economy that has placed significant rewards on simply getting our attention in a growingly crowded and noisy news space. Facts need not apply. Salacious and altogether false headlines drive clicks, which drive the sale of Toyotas and toaster ovens. Thus, when setting up our DEL environments we must encourage the use of credible sources.

One way that educators can protect themselves from fake news sources is to pay for a subscription to more credible sources. In some cases, a strategic investment in a resource data bank will pay significant dividends in terms of the richness of the content. Getting connected, for example, to the local public library or a university database can be helpful.

Understand That Your Students Are Digital Natives

Digital natives—people who've grown up in a digital world—show a consistent willingness to go online via social networking spaces and interact with other experienced users of the resource to determine if it will be of value to them (Guest, 2015). In most cases, these users are not known to the digital native and half or more of them live outside of the United States. For example, before making reservations at a hotel, many consult individual reviews on TripAdvisor. Before making a decision to get a haircut at a local salon, people consult Yelp reviews. For the criticism millennials and Generation Z often endure, this is a strong indicator that these up-and-coming generations are conscious of the integrity and variety of resources that exist in the digital world. Therefore, it is incumbent on facilitators to provide students with reputable, and quality resources that extend their learning in dynamic ways. They are already connecting with others, and all kinds of outside materials, thus facilitators must find ways to point them to the right resources.

As such, suggesting certain Twitter feeds, Kahn Academy tutorials, Facebook feeds (like NPR), and so on puts them on the right path to finding the most reputable and timely information available to bolster their acumen for connecting with each other and finding quality and helpful resources to support new learning and innovation.

As you select your resources and content, also provide a content overview for the course and articulate why the course is important to your learners. This is not as important at elementary-grade levels where students are generally accepting of the curriculum you dictate, but at middle- and higher-grade levels, establishing this sense of purpose helps get your students to buy into your curriculum. Figure 3.3 includes an example of a content overview for a grade 6 social studies class.

Greetings Everyone,

Welcome to sixth-grade social studies! We have an exciting year ahead of us! This year, we will be learning about ancient Greece and Rome, focusing mostly on key wars and leaders. Studying these two cultures will help you gain an understanding of how ideas about democracy were born. We will continue our study of our historical roots by examining the underpinnings of industrialism, capitalism, and socialism. During this unit, we will engage in debate and create a mock society. In addition, we will explore aspects of immigration, industrialization, and urbanization, as well as women's and African American rights reform movements and initiatives. Understanding our historical roots is helpful for making better decisions for governing society in a manner that is in keeping with democratic principles established through the U.S. Bill of Rights, Constitution, and its amendments. Hopefully, through the study of these topics, you will feel more empowered as a citizen of the United States and will be better equipped to someday directly engage in the democratic process. I look forward to working with each of you on this journey!

Ms. Smith

Figure 3.3: Sample course content overview.

Once you establish the purpose and scope of your online learning course via a quick introduction to your students, it's time to explain to your students the expectations for that course.

Create Regular Office Hours

It is important to create regular office hours and organize time for synchronous availability. In most traditional digital learning experiences, instructors try to establish virtual office hours during which they make themselves available in multiple ways. They may identify times of the day throughout the week during which they are working online and are available to answer questions, either via phone call, email, or instant message, depending on the system. In most cases your LMS platform provides tools for this purpose, while in scenarios you might use your own solution, such as Skype or Google Hangouts. This is helpful because there are students who inevitably need assistance, and being able to count on your availability allows them to access the most important resource of all, the instructor. It may be helpful to set up office hours at a variety of times throughout the week to allow students with different schedules to connect with you. It is also beneficial to let learners know that if they are not available during the times you have posted, you will arrange a day and time that accommodates their needs.

Establish Expectations for Facilitator-to-Learner Interaction

When drafting your course overview, from introduction and resource gathering to establishing office hours, bear in mind that every institution has an administrative policy to meet digital quality standards but that this is simply the minimal expectation. You should supplement the learning experience and parameters for the learners based on your classroom management style to best support your relationship with learners and to ensure a safe and productive classroom experience. Therefore, in your expectations, you should explain three elements: (1) what learners can expect of you, (2) what you expect of them, and (3) what their expectations should be of each other. Let's look at each of these items in turn.

What Learners Can Expect of You

Learners need to know that you are committed to their success and growth. Learners also need to know what they can expect in terms of how soon you will provide feedback on their assignments, how quickly you will answer questions via email or another modality, and what you are committed to offer them in terms of support and assistance. Basically, they require assurances of you as a facilitator to their learning. Figure 3.4 (page 50) shows an example of what you might say within a *faculty expectations post*, which is a message you post to the LMS platform at the start of the course.

- I will answer all questions sent asynchronously within twenty-four hours on weekdays and forty-eight hours on weekends and holidays.

- I will provide support and resources to help you meet learning goals.

- I will let you know via email and announcements if I have to reschedule a class meeting or cannot provide you with feedback on your assignments within seventy-two hours of submission.

- My office hours are . . .

Figure 3.4: List of expectations students may have of the facilitator.

Once you establish what your learners can expect of you, you can move on to what you expect of them.

What You Expect of Learners

It is vital to the learning experience that you explain what you expect from your students in terms of their overall behavior, how they interact with you, and what they will accomplish within the course. Setting up these guidelines assists learners in better navigating interaction and communication within the classroom. Students need to understand what is expected of them in the class, what specific instructions for communication they should follow, and appropriate netiquette. This will help you set up a class that is conducive to productive learning growth and engagement. Figure 3.5 offers an example of what you might post for student expectations.

- Identify personal goals for this course, and work toward achieving them.

- Ask questions when you don't understand something or need extra help.

- Read through all the assigned resources, and make sure you are prepared to practice concepts and skills throughout the course.

- Make sure all correspondence with me and your peers is professional, polite, and focused on problem solving. If you have a question or concern, before you correspond with me, try to think of at least one solution to the problem, and then communicate that to me along with your question or concern.

- Take the initiative to find information and resources related to your goals and what we are studying.

- Attend all required classroom meetings and communicate with me if you run into problems with attendance or turning in your work or have trouble with a concept. You can simply send me an email to let me know or contact me during office hours if you need to talk live.

- Offer additional resources and ideas about everything we cover in class. This is a class where we are not only studying topics, but we are also building and even creating knowledge. Feel free to add new information, ideas, and solutions to all problems and topics we explore in this course.

- Turn in all work by the assigned deadline. If something comes up and you cannot make the deadline, be sure to communicate with me ahead of time. Please know that work submitted late may incur deductions.

- Read through, use, and ask questions as needed on the feedback you receive.

- When contacting me during office hours, make sure that you are prepared with at least two specific questions to which you need answers. Do not simply say, "I don't know how to do this." You must ask specific questions about the concept or direction that requires clarification. For example, you might say, "I want to write about butterflies, but I cannot think of a topic around that concept that is arguable. Can you help me think of something?" or "I want to write about the possible extinction of bees, but I can't think of three main points to cover within my paper that will help me show what needs to be done to prevent their extinction. Can you help me find some sources or brainstorm for some ideas as to where I can look to identify three possible solutions to the problem?"

Figure 3.5: List of expectations you have of your learners.

Guidelines like these will set you on the path to establishing positive, constructive discourse with your students. The next step is to ensure your students can have the same sort of experience when communicating with each other.

What Learners Should Expect of Each Other

Teaching learners how to interact with each other is imperative to supporting lively, deep, and rich conversations and learning experiences in the classroom. Learners are not born knowing how to interact with each other and are likely to interact with each other very differently through informal social networking and other digital venues than they would in the real world. Therefore, establishing guidelines and giving examples for how to interact with each other online will help them make the transition from the more informal digital communication modalities to the more formal and professional modality. Figure 3.6 provides an example of what you might post.

Greetings Class,

I want to take some time to discuss with you some guidelines for interacting with each other in the classroom. Following these guidelines will not only help us stay focused on what is important in the class but also help you maintain positive relationships with your peers.

- Always be professional, be polite, and talk with others in a respectful tone.

- Never send anything when you are angry. Think through what you want to say before sending it, because you can't take back what you send—it is permanent. Therefore, when you feel frustrated or upset, write down your thoughts. Then put them aside for an hour or so, and come back to them. Then revise what you wrote so that you are communicating what you want to know or understand from the conversation rather than communicating your anger or frustration. Think about what you want out of the correspondence. What is the outcome you desire? Facilitating that outcome means making sure you stick to clarifying the primary issue and asking for that instead of venting your frustrations.

- If you are not sure what someone meant, ask for clarification before assuming what he or she meant to say.

- Remember that everyone has a bad day sometimes. Try to be forgiving if conflict does arise. We are here to learn and grow together, not fight.

- Remember that it is OK to agree to disagree. We are not always going to reach consensus. It's OK not to agree and say so.

- If you have any questions and want to run something past me before corresponding with your peers, you are welcome to do so.

For example, if you feel as though your team or group is not using your input in a class project, you might post something like this:

> *Dear Mike, Sarah, and Tim,*
>
> *I gave you an idea yesterday, but I don't see it in the project. It was an explanation of how to . . . I think it will be useful because . . . Do you think we can use it?*
>
> *Thanks,*
>
> *Mary*
>
> This keeps the discussion civil and allows the other group members to say either they didn't receive the idea or provide a reason for not using the idea.
>
> Please let me know if you have any questions about this. I am here to help!
>
> Ms. Smith

Figure 3.6: List of guidelines for peer-to-peer communication.

Establishing your expectations for classroom interactions at all levels is just the start of building a positive online learning environment for your learners. Ensuring that they have a firm grasp of what is permissible in their work and how to assemble it is paramount.

Provide Information on Academic Honesty and Digital Citizenship

Students need to understand the tenets of academic honesty, including the school's code of conduct for students, rules about plagiarism, and how to cite sources and information properly and why it's beneficial to them to do so. It is also important that learners understand established technology guidelines, like how to safely surf the web and how to find safe sources (those that are not corrupted with viruses or malware or are misleading). This includes ensuring students understand the ramifications of their own behavior in online spaces. They must know what is required of them to be good digital citizens and how what they say in public forums, in many cases, cannot ever be removed. Read Matt Davis's (2016) "Digital Citizenship Week: 6 Resources for Educators" (http://edut.to/2iz6Vz9) to learn more about establishing digital citizenship guidelines.

Send a Welcome Message

Whenever possible, it is helpful to contact learners before the beginning of the course. Sending out a welcome message, like the one in figure 3.7 (page 54), one to two weeks before the course starts and beginning a friendly threaded dialogue in that space sets a positive tone, letting learners know that you are invested in them and their progress (Keengwe, Adjei-Boateng, & Diteeyont, 2013).

Greetings!

I am John Smith, your teacher for English 1, and I am excited to be working with you on this journey! In this class, we cover American literature, British literature, poetry, and several genres of writing, including expository, persuasive, and narrative. We will also do some research writing and engage in a mock debate, and you will work on many other projects with your classmates. If you have any questions you'd like to ask about me or this course, please go ahead and post them in this thread, and I'll make sure to answer.

The focus in my class is on pursuing your interests and deeply exploring topics so that you can use what you learn in your own life. You might ask, "How do these concepts apply to my life?" The course is set up to show you just how you can use, apply, and relate the concepts to your own life. For example, the way in which the main character in a story handles a situation might teach you how to handle a similar situation in your own life. Therefore, to set up a personalized learning environment for you and help you get the most out of this course, I'd like to learn more about you. Please take a moment to answer the following questions and send your answers back to me via email. I look forward to working with you!

- What are your general hobbies and interests? What do you like to do in your free time?
- What have been your experiences in writing? What are your strengths? What are your fears?
- What do you like to read (poetry, true stories, fiction, books, magazines, and so on)?
- What is your best time of day for working? When do you feel the most awake and alert?
- What job do you want to do when you grow up?
- What is your favorite subject, and why?
- What do you like about working with classmates?
- What do you dislike about working with classmates?
- What types of problems do you like to solve?

Figure 3.7: Sample welcome message to engage students in your class.

Notice the request in this message for your students to contact you directly with information about themselves. As you receive responses from your class, we recommend contacting learners individually to engage more directly with them. Where your group message may contain various details regarding the upcoming learning experience, your initial learner contact may be a simple and less formal note to let each learner know you are approachable and interested in his or her success as a student. Use the information he or she responds with, or details gleaned from your classroom's threaded dialogue, to establish a personalized connection with each learner (see figure 3.8).

Hello, Tony!

Welcome to my English 1 class! Make sure you read all of my announcements this week, which detail course expectations and week one assignments. I read that you have a Labrador retriever. I grew up with a yellow Lab that we called Golden. He was the best dog! Have you had any other types of dogs?

I'm looking forward to working with you, and welcome again to English 1!

Mr. Smith

Figure 3.8: Sample personalized note to a learner.

After you initiate contact with your students, another step you can take to increase learners' comfort level with your course is to allow them to log in to the course early and have a look around. This allows those who might need a head start the opportunity to get in and get comfortable.

Post *Start Here* Announcements

Although your LMS may depend to some degree on internal email, you will likely have a discussion board where you can post administrative announcements. We recommend you post a *start here* announcement, like the one in figure 3.9 (page 56), to advise the learners where to go or what to do first. This is different from your initial welcome and course overview posts. This is less about the course curriculum and more about helping students engage with LMS's intricacies.

Greetings!

It is a great pleasure to be working with all of you in this course! I do look forward to our work together as we explore the material presented. In order to get started, it is important that you read through the material located in the People area, where you can find information about me. You can also go the Syllabus to find information about the course, including what we will study and when, as well as teacher, learner, and peer-to-peer communication expectations. Also, be sure to familiarize yourself with all of the materials and assignments offered within this course. I encourage you to use the calendar template to schedule time to work on assignments. The calendar already notes due dates for assignments, discussions, and projects. Once you have completed the aforementioned tasks, be sure to let me know by posting that you have done so under this thread. I look forward to learning with you on this journey!

Mr. Smith

Figure 3.9: Start here announcement.

Although it's true that most digital natives in K–12 education already have a relatively high degree of technical aptitude and the ability to navigate a virtual learning space with ease, your students will appreciate the thoughtful nature of a message like this one.

Make Learning and Performance Expectations Clear

Making learning and performance expectations explicitly clear is one of the more important steps you can take in an online learning environment. This includes, but is not limited to, the identification of major assignments, assessment expectations and how they are weighted, and whenever possible, the presentation of learning rubrics. Although learning online has several pedagogical advantages, the opportunity for communication or translation breakdown is still there. For example, if you communicate to your students that the goal of a project on Newton's laws of motion is to effectively demonstrate how each law works in a practical manner, but the grading criteria places heavy emphasis on creativity of the video students are to produce, then students will become confused about the expectations for the assignment or project and may not fully engage, or not engage at all. Such an outcome may cause a majority of students to fail to reach the assignment's goal. As a result, the more explicit you can be about proficiency expectations, the better (Brookhart, 2013).

Close Technology Gaps

Even though we are living in a high-tech world, there are still families who do not have access to even the most basic hardware, software, and networking capabilities that make learning online possible. Part of the reason learning platforms have, historically, been relatively simple is because there is such a wide variance in user capability. Without question, it is essential to create a learning experience for everyone to enjoy. Although most schools ensure students and parents are aware of major technological requirements at the time of enrollment, if your posts require extra downloads of applications or certain video capabilities, be aware that some of your students may not have access to the tools necessary to enjoy those experiences. We do not necessarily recommend that you refrain from applying these tools. We do suggest, however, that you apply them carefully and reach out to your students to determine if these gaps exist. If so, you can work with these particular students when these technology challenges emerge.

Other Dos and Don'ts of Online Learning

A lot of critical work goes into establishing and organizing your online learning curriculum. The advice in this chapter should get you off to a proper start, but it's important that you stay organized in your practices as the course moves forward. In this section, we highlight some of the more critical dos and don'ts you should consider in facilitating your students' education.

Avoid Posting Too Much Content at Once

While engaged in a complex instructional design concept, we worked with editors who marveled at the over two hundred pages of content we hoped to post in the virtual learning space. They were surprised and asked, "You can get the students to read all of that information?" Their implication was quite right. Students in K–12 would find a two-hundred-page document daunting, and it is highly unlikely they would read it at all. This is despite the fact that we designed this particular course to gradually release each unit of instruction, so the students could experience the content little by little.

The message in this apparent contradiction is that students are more likely to consume large amounts of content if you share it with them in shorter, more digestible portions. Thus, we recommend that you do not post all your course content at once. Also, if possible, keep your announcements short. This is also true of videos, as we discuss later in this chapter. Although there may be some instances in which a longer viewing is required, a simple perusal of YouTube videos indicates that the most popular videos are ninety seconds or less. There are many reasons for this, but the simplest is that we prefer digital content in smaller servings. Keep this in mind as you prepare your learning experience.

Establish an Inviting, Caring, and Enthusiastic Tone

Tone is important in any online learning experience. Many of you reading this book may remember receiving an email or text message from a friend and sensing she was in a bad mood or that something was wrong. Simple steps, such as beginning every announcement with a friendly greeting (like, "Hello"), and generous use of exclamation points and other positive affirmations, go a long way in creating a positive, energizing tone. Although many instructors in a face-to-face learning environment consistently provide tone-enhancing affirmations via physical gestures, such as smiling and laughing, these cues simply are not possible in an online learning space (unless you're communicating via video, of course). As a result, it is advantageous to ensure your correspondence conveys a friendly, positive, personalized, and interested tone.

Be Considerate of Students With Learning Challenges and Disabilities

We strongly recommend that, as a facilitator, you consider providing learners with specialized links to resources and offer applicable learning alternatives to them if they have a disability or any other hindrance to learning, such as a broken hand or arm. For example, devices such as screen readers, closed-captioned translators, and video transcripts are often available to students. Some learners make use of speech software, such as Dragon NaturallySpeaking, while others listen to recorded books due to vision or hearing problems as well as other reading impediments like dyslexia.

Post an Audio or a Video Clip

When introducing yourself to students in writing, keep in mind that many learners also appreciate a short welcome video or audio clip (one to two minutes) that brings to life your expertise and presence in the classroom. Audio and video provide added advantages by allowing students to see you and hear you, further personalizing the learning experience. You can extend this thinking beyond your initial welcome message. Classroom tours, including video or screenshots that describe different aspects of the course and how to access course features, are another positive contribution. Posting these items in the introduction section sometimes means restating much of what is already written in your introduction, syllabus, and course expectations, but rather than being repetitive, this generally serves to reinforce this information for students.

Conclusion

The steps you take to set up your online learning experience will undoubtedly pay dividends throughout the course. If you have not had the opportunity to launch a virtual learning course before, you will learn as you go, just like any new teaching experience. The information in this chapter will serve you well in understanding LMS platforms and how you can keep a course organized within them. During the launch cycle, we urge you to take notes on the steps that worked, as well as the challenges you met, so you can adjust the next time you teach the class. In the next chapter, we address the steps you can take to kick off your class and provide your students with a great start.

CHAPTER 4

Initiating the Learning Experience

In this chapter, we examine the steps that modern facilitators take in kicking off the DEL experience and introducing learners to their virtual learning course room. Just like any learning experience, a strong start makes a difference! After taking the steps articulated in chapter 3 to prepare the learning experience, this chapter focuses on what to do as your learners log in and get started.

KEY QUESTIONS ANSWERED IN THIS CHAPTER

- How do you create a foundation that establishes a partnership between what learners want to learn and what the course offers?

- How can you assess and support the diverse needs of learners in your classroom?

- How can you engage with each learner and provide resources that facilitate a continuous connection between his or her understanding and content?

- How can you make learners feel comfortable in a communal learning environment?

- How can you help learners engage with each other and feel excited about learning in your classroom?

The adage that you never get a second chance to make a good first impression is true. From a learning standpoint, our initial exposure to something births a cognitive precept that forms initial thoughts, feelings, and overall levels of engagement and connection. With that in mind, let's examine some important foundations you can establish for your online classroom.

Foundations for Learning in Your Classroom

Although a strong start in any teaching, training, or coaching environment is important, it's especially essential when conducting learning experiences related to DEL. After a bad start in a face-to-face meeting, you may be able to reshape the momentum with a warm and engaging presence and some healthy exchanges. In online learning environments, the first impression isn't measured by the first moments eyeballs find one another. Instead, it's driven by a multitude of factors that include the degree to which the LMS appears inviting and the initial connections facilitators make with students to ensure a strong start is underway.

We talked in detail in chapter 3 about the importance of early communication with your class, as a group and as individuals, before it starts. As your class gets underway, it's critical to assess what your students already know. There are strategies you can employ to gain a deeper understanding of the knowledge your students bring to the class, including the use of preassessments, that you can then use to help move them smoothly into the flow of your curriculum.

Preassessments

In many cases, prepackaged course curricula offer preassessment tools. If your course does not already offer a preassessment, however, you still have options. Discover your learners' interests and prior knowledge by creating an entry ticket to the course requesting that each learner identify what he or she already knows and what he or she wants to learn from the course. You can also create a short survey asking learners to self-assess their level of knowledge on the content to be covered. This could be a short survey of three to five questions, but it should be designed to help you assess what learners know and can do regarding the subject matter. Preassessments and self-assessments also help learners think about the subject matter in a deeper way.

Gathering preliminary information on existing levels of student proficiency may be helpful at all levels and with all modalities, but it's particularly informative with DEL. First, depending on how they are designed, preassessments can provide you with a glimpse of learner preferences, prior knowledge, work preferences, and so on. This can assist in your ability to help them make deeper connections with the subject matter. Second, and perhaps even more important, is that by gathering information about each learner, you can then determine how much preinstruction and enrichment are necessary to help every learner grow in the subject matter. As you identify specific skill gaps, the DEL modality allows you to do more with that information than might otherwise be possible.

For example, if you have students answer three questions about their knowledge of the Civil War, you might find out that over half of the students have already covered certain aspects that are baked into the course. Instead of having learners simply repeat those concepts, you tweak the learning assignments just a bit, adding some resources and even some additional learning options, to extend their knowledge. Conversely, if you find that learners have learned nothing in previous courses about the Civil War, and the learning tasks in the class are too advanced for their current knowledge state, you might elect to provide some remedial information and resources to get them caught up so they can successfully engage in the content of the course.

HELPING STUDENTS CATCH UP

Research shows that facilitators in online classes often make assumptions about learners' prerequisite knowledge and do not provide detailed explanations of concepts. When facilitators provide a plethora of examples and links to resources to assist learners, they are better able to connect lacking skills and information to subskills (Mayes, Luebeck, Ku, Akarasriworn, & Korkmaz, 2011).

Suffice it to say, preassessments and self-assessments create an atmosphere of deep reflection and self-evaluation, and they help you know where to start in the learning process. As you collect data, consider creating a chart like the one in figure 4.1 that lists each learner and his or her current comfort level with the subject matter as well as the student's interests and needs.

Student	Prior Knowledge Pretest	Specific Areas of Deficit	Specific Areas of Strength	Areas of Interest and Special Needs
Sally	3/10	Influences on Civil War, U.S. Constitution, leaders	Significance of and outcomes	What people were like during the Civil War period and the real reason behind the Civil War; needs reminders to stay on task in group work
Tom	8/10	U.S. Constitution	Significance of and outcomes, influences of Civil War, and leadership	How the Civil War influences life today, leaders of the Civil War and their impact
Mike	7/10	Influences on Civil War	Significance of and outcomes, U.S. Constitution	Battle locations and outcomes; needs extra time to finish projects; must use the computer to produce written work

Figure 4.1: Learner data chart.

In addition to creating a chart like this, consider drafting notes on each learner you can have open as you interact with and assess him or her. If your LMS platform doesn't provide a function for this purpose, there are free tools like Microsoft OneNote and Evernote that work extremely well.

Whatever method you use to keep track of learner data, having such information easily accessible when corresponding with students and tailoring instruction to meet their needs will prove invaluable to bolstering their engagement in the learning process.

Goal Setting and Strategies

It is important to explain the goals of the course to learners so that they have a foundational understanding of the intent and expectations of the course and each lesson. This combats the possibility of them seeing the work as meaningless busywork. There are multiple strategies you can employ in articulating course goals in a way that not only engages your students but also allows you to understand the goals better. The better you know your own course's ambitions, the better equipped you are to ensure learners will meet and exceed these goals. We endorse a three-step process: (1) conveying course goals to learners, (2) having learners set their personal goals for the course, and (3) meshing learner and course goals.

Convey Goals to Learners

The simplest approach to setting goals is to convey them directly to your learners. For example, the goal may be to develop reading fluency, comprehension, and decoding skills, as well as writing fluency and process skills. Communicating this to learners at the beginning of the course and then continuing to do so for each lesson throughout the course lets them know what to expect (see figure 4.2).

Greetings Class,

I know that many of you have asked, "Why do we need to learn how to write an essay? I am never going to write an essay in the job I want to do." Well, that is a great question to ask, and while you may not write a formal five-paragraph essay in the job that you want to do, someday you will very likely have to write a work report or an email defending a decision you made within the scope of your job. To obtain employment, you will have to write a cover letter that convinces a potential employer that you are the best candidate for the job. In addition, you may have to write an email or letter to a vendor contesting or disputing a fraudulent charge made in your name. You may have to write an email or memo to an employee to help the employee do a better job or to communicate some new protocol or practice that employees will be expected to implement in their areas of expertise.

These are just a few of the ways in which you may communicate in writing. Learning how to generate ideas, organize ideas, and communicate those ideas in a clear and understandable way enable you to find success in those endeavors. Therefore, for this next project, you will be asked to work together to come up with a strategy for completing some type of task in thirty minutes or less. The goal of the project is for you to come up with a protocol for completing some type of task in an effective and efficient manner. You are going to, as a team, write an essay providing someone with directions for completing the task in less than thirty minutes. In other words, you should go through the entire writing process with your team to provide a step-by-step, detailed explanation as to how to do something. It can be how to wash a car, how to change someone's mind, how to clean the house, and so on, in thirty minutes or less.

Good luck!

Mr. Jones

Figure 4.2: Sample communication of goals.

If you are going to have students create a process essay, as in this example, reminding students that one course goal is to develop writing fluency and process skills and then stating performance objectives (for example, students will engage fully in the writing process in order to generate a polished five-paragraph process essay), or *I can* statements (such as *I can brainstorm for ideas in order to write a process essay; I can edit multiple drafts in order to create a polished process essay*) for the lesson gives them a solid foundation on which they can focus, hone their skills, and develop knowledge about that target area.

While initiating the learning experience, there is an opportunity for the facilitator to give a course overview and explain how each module will impact the students' learning—facilitators can offer a video or an auditory overview to explain how the course might help students.

Have Learners Set Personal Course Goals

Facilitators can also set up an initial discussion thread to help students understand what they need to learn about the subject matter and establish their own goals for the course. Have learners create and share personal goals. This helps learners better connect with the subject matter, bringing clarity about subject matter meaning to their learning.

When asking learners to create goals, you need to offer them some direction and guidance. This is why engaging them in a discussion about the tenets of the course may help them (see figure 4.3). Offer students your own insights, direct them to read those explanations, and lead them to create and share goals.

Greetings Class,

You might ask yourself, "Why do I need to read about these topics, and why do I need to do all of this writing for this class? How will it help me in my life?" Consider that much of how you talk with one another in the digital age is through the written word (text, email, and so on), and given that many of you will have jobs someday that will require you to write reports, evaluations, updates, memos, and so on, good writing skills are important. In addition, with all the information available today through the Internet, you also need to be able to determine what information is credible, dependable, and believable. Therefore, learning how to read about information and how to determine if it's worthy of reading is important. In addition, all the literature we will read this year provides important messages and insights that might help you navigate problems, issues, and decisions in your own life. Exploring these texts may help you make better informed decisions in your own lives. As such, I would like for you to read through the syllabus and then come up with two or three goals you would like to achieve in this course and share them with the class. In your response to your peers, feel free to ask questions or discuss how their goals are similar to or different from yours. I look forward to reading about your goals!

Mr. Jones

Figure 4.3: Example of facilitating the construction of personal course goals.

When learners articulate their personal goals, they solidify, confirm, and affirm those goals, directing their brain to focus on them. In addition, articulating personal goals for the course helps them determine the course's relevance in their own lives and prompts them to take responsibility for, and ownership over, their own learning. Having them create goals also helps you, as the facilitator, best serve the learners and gain insight into their interests and needs, which enhances their learning at the highest level.

Mesh Learner and Course Goals

When we show learners how their goals and interests align with the course goals, we help them see the relevance of their work in the course and provide them with a more meaningful course experience. This provides learners with a forward-thinking perspective of how they might apply the subject matter in their own lives, now and in the future (see figure 4.4).

Greetings Everyone,

In looking over the poll I posted this morning, I noticed that most of you do a lot of texting and messaging online. You said that you get frustrated when someone misinterprets what you say in your messages. The good news is, this next unit will provide you with some valuable tips, tools, and practice for better ensuring that what you convey in written words is clear! In particular, we will work on the organization of your ideas, using precise words and solid sentence structure. I think you are going to enjoy this next unit we will cover, and I believe you will come away with new (or polished) skills for better ensuring that your messages are interpreted correctly from now on.

Mr. Jones

Figure 4.4: Example of aligning course goals and learner goals.

Engaging students on both course and personal levels helps them see the relevance of what they are learning and prompts them to engage in the new learning with a greater level of enthusiasm and earnest effort. Once you engage students in the goals they need to meet, you can start engaging them in the actual process of learning.

Continuous Engagement

In the previous chapter, we discussed the importance of introducing yourself to your students. This process of active engagement doesn't end when the class begins. As a digital facilitator, it's critical that you continuously take every step possible to demonstrate a high level of active, interested engagement by ensuring that learners notice your presence when they log in. For example, under a posted discussion question, there should be a personal note from you inviting students to engage in the discussion. If learners start to ask questions in public places, it is essential that you provide active responses to let them know that you are paying attention to what is going on and will quickly answer questions. By acting like you're the host of the party, circulating the room and making sure everyone feels welcome, you ensure that the learning experience feels more authentic.

Let's take a look at some of the primary ways you can increase engagement among your students.

Facilitate Threaded Discussions

Now that your learners have entered the learning space, and you have given them the direction to collaborate and respond, you will see what we refer to as *threaded discussions* begin to emerge. We use the term *thread* because we navigate most online conversations by scrolling down and reading through back-and-forth commentary between participants. If you have a friend who sends you text messages regularly, and you save those texts, you can scroll back and observe a link to a threaded discussion, possibly one posted months, or even years, prior.

Over the next several chapters we talk a lot about digital teaming and the ability to create thoughtful conversations in cyber-asynchronous learning environments. This is ultimately about creating dynamic discussions in digital classrooms that are rich, stimulating, and engaging. Throughout this book, you will consistently see references to ongoing, threaded discussions in your digital classroom. Your goal, as a facilitator, is to set up a class and inspire engaging threads—the kind of discussions that push the conversation forward and help students develop their thinking.

Engage Through Resources

You can use resources to provoke engagement. Research shows that when learners receive information in a variety of contexts, specifically in both visual and audio formats, they learn and retain that content to a greater degree (Mayes et al., 2011). Therefore, consider adding audiovisual media to the course, but do so sparingly and in limited capacity. Whereas your video messages to students should be restricted to just a few minutes, when selecting audiovisual media you have more flexibility in length— target twenty- to thirty-minute segments. You can use such materials to introduce or wrap up concepts or offer expertise on the subject matter. Digital standards for accessibility require closed-captioning at the highest accessibility level, but at the least, a text version of the audiovisual content can serve learners with hearing or visual impairments (Web Accessibility Initiative, 2012).

Furthermore, consider using asynchronous and synchronous tools to support learner and facilitator interaction. Synchronous tools, such as Google Hangouts,

Zoom, Adobe Connect, and Second Life, can motivate learners to stay engaged, help them sustain the same pace as their colleagues, increase their feelings of connectedness to the class and each other, and offer them immediate feedback (Yuan & Kim, 2014). Note that synchronous tools are only useful if the facilitator appropriately manages them. Therefore, it is wise to use preassessment data to provide multiple options to different groups (Hockett & Doubet, 2013). You should also consider scaffolding lessons and grouping learners to ensure they are learning at their own pace and have adequate support from each other to grapple with key concepts.

Because using just one chat session to facilitate conversation among multiple groups can quickly break down, it is also a good idea to provide group lessons in separate chat sessions to ensure success. For example, after conducting a prior-knowledge and interest-inventory survey, you could create digital learning centers that specifically call out key areas that students should learn to become proficient in. Consider opportunities for remediation and enrichment and target areas of personal interest for learners when creating the centers (King-Sears, 2007).

Offering opportunities for students to engage in new learning using a variety of process, product, and content modalities stimulates engagement as well (Manning, Standford, & Reeves, 2010). For example, in referring to the chart in figure 4.1 (page 63), you might create one learning center that engages learners in understanding some of the influences and outcomes of the Civil War, giving students choices regarding how they want to interact with the subject matter, such as creating a group research paper, coordinating and participating in a mock debate on the discussion board, or designing a plan for stopping the war. Another learning center could focus on the influence of the U.S. Constitution on decision making during the war. Within this center, learners could engage in a poster session in which they identify and present these influences to each other either through video presentations or through a discussion forum. Still another option is to have learners engage in a literature circle wherein the group reads a book and then discusses and debates its message, such as what aspects of the book do or do not support the notion that the U.S. Constitution influenced decision making during the Civil War. You can scaffold learning within these centers by offering students links to information, videos, and so on, as well as checkpoints, tests, and self-assessments that ensure students acquire the knowledge they need to complete the application tasks.

Figure 4.5 (page 70) offers another example of scaffolding content and assignments.

Sample Learning Objectives by Lesson	Sample Assignment
Lesson 1: Learners will be able to recognize the different quadrilateral shapes.	Create an infographic identifying all the quadrilateral shapes shared in this lesson.
Lesson 2: Learners will be able to make connections between similar and different properties of quadrilateral shapes.	Create a visual that shows how each of the quadrilaterals is similar to and different from the others based on their properties. Make sure that you match each of the quadrilaterals with each of the others.
Lesson 3: Learners will be able to identify quadrilateral shapes based on given properties.	Create a quiz for a partner. In this quiz, provide your partner with the properties of a quadrilateral and ask him or her to match it to the correct answer in an answer key.
Summative Assessment	
Combine your parts for lessons 1 to 3, incorporating all the feedback your teacher has provided. Share this with your partner (without the answer key). Complete your partner's assessment using his or her work as your guide, and turn it in to your teacher. Your teacher will call you and discuss your summative assessment, offering a verbal assessment to follow as well as your unit test.	

Figure 4.5: Scaffolding content and assignments.

Provide Alternate Resources and Access

Because learners engage best with content in different formats, we recommend that you offer learners a variety of resources and options for learning the material. Note that the material must be clearly connected to the content you cover. If course content is already uploaded, allow for alternative assignments. For example, a learner may not feel comfortable creating a video of him- or herself (or for religious reasons cannot do so), so give him or her the option to create an audio presentation or even a written presentation.

We also suggest that you gradually release resources as they connect to course content. Scaffold information to ensure that learners are challenged at the right level and pace. Offer remediation and enrichment exercises, materials, and resources so that students can extend their learning (Song, Wong, & Looi, 2012).

The gradual release of materials to students can occur in many ways depending on the technology available and student needs. For example, if a system has gradual release capabilities, then a teacher can release content based on the standard as determined by mastery of diagnostic test items. If a teacher would simply like to release a lesson or a module at a time, most LMSs have this capability based on either calendar entries or through manual control over when to show or hide content.

What if the system does not have these capabilities? This question requires some reflection back to our brick-and-mortar classrooms. When a school year begins, most if not all materials are in the classroom. The teacher simply takes out what he or she would like to use that day and focuses students on that resource. The online classroom is the same. Teachers can achieve the same effect using announcements and other forms of communication to direct students.

Regardless of method, every resource you provide should be easily accessible, and it should be clear why you selected it. Everything needs to be connected to what you are attempting to teach—the product, process, and content all need to be connected to the goals and objectives for the new learning (Song et al., 2012). Learners become disengaged if they don't see the relevance in what they are doing or perceive the work to be busywork (Snyder & Linnenbrink-Garcia, 2013).

Establish a Community Mindset

Human beings learn more when they work together in communities of practice and application (DuFour & Reason, 2016). Thus, the degree to which you can establish a positive, affirming, rigorous, and engaging learning community drives a learner's ability to enjoy your online learning class. Once again, this is not dissimilar from the steps you must take in a face-to-face classroom. The strategies in this space, however, are a bit different. To some degree, you must be a bit more overt about taking direct steps to get learners to connect with each other and to make sure that the type of community you expect begins to evolve. If you choose to create a synchronous initial collaborative experience, consider making the session as short as possible, factoring in the number of learners in attendance, start-up time, and ending time for questions. For example, if you have a small group of learners, this session could be as short as twenty minutes, whereas if you have a large group of learners, it may be best to provide thirty minutes. Be mindful of learners who come in late. Stop and say, "Hello," but keep the momentum with the session.

If the session is asynchronous, consider the use of discussion forums. Despite the format, forums provide valuable information for you as the facilitator. For example, by reading through their dialogue, you can determine if students understand the content and are able to extend and apply the new learning. This is a key time to redirect, remediate, or provide extended learning opportunities.

Knowing more about your learners will help in conflict management, learner engagement, and course success. Here are a few suggestions for synchronous and asynchronous environments that we like to use in the initial engagement of an online learning space to help break the ice, build community, and establish communication patterns that will help make your course successful.

- **Live-chat icebreakers:** There are strategies you can deploy in a live chat that act as icebreakers for your students.

  - Before the chat, send out an email asking learners to create a short introduction of themselves in which they come up with an adjective that describes who they are and put that adjective in front of their name. Then ask them to come up with one sentence that explains why that adjective best represents them. When learners enter the room, they should write their adjective name and a one-sentence explanation in the conversation box. For example, a learner might write, "Hi, I am athletic Tina, because I love to play basketball," or "I am happy Mike, because I am always smiling." When the chat starts, give each learner one minute to describe why the adjective describes him or her and give the other students two minutes to ask that student questions about the adjective he or she selected.

  - When learners enter the chat room, greet them personally and have them participate in a poll or vote. For example, you might have learners vote on their favorite movie, song, or television show. Then ask learners to introduce themselves by stating their name and their vote by either using the conversation box or granting them presentation privileges in the LMS. They can then state an alternative favorite movie or song if it wasn't on the list you provided.

  - When learners enter the chat room, pair each with another student. Have the pairs interview each other for three to five minutes, and then give each student one minute to introduce his or her partner to the class. You can have students do this by giving them presenter privileges or by having them write out their introductions in the conversation box. While learners are interviewing each other, establish the order in which they will introduce each other and post it to the chat.

    Be sure to end a virtual synchronous chat by thanking students for participating and directing them to the first deliverable for the course—for example, "Thank you all for sharing. I really enjoyed meeting all of you! Be sure to go through the syllabus to familiarize yourself with the course and then go to the first module and read through the directions for the activity. Let me know via email, instant message or phone call if you have any questions."

- **Collage icebreaker:** Creating a collage or an electronic bulletin board of your background allows students another opportunity to get to know you. Encourage students to do the same and to post during the collaborative experience. Examples of this may be pictures and links to items that represent elements of their lives. Allow students to include a written or auditory narrative of the tour for increased interaction. This can be done directly in the course room or through a program such as VoiceThread. Many additional tools exist on the Internet to create collages. One of these, pictured in figure 4.6 is a Wordle (www.wordle.net).

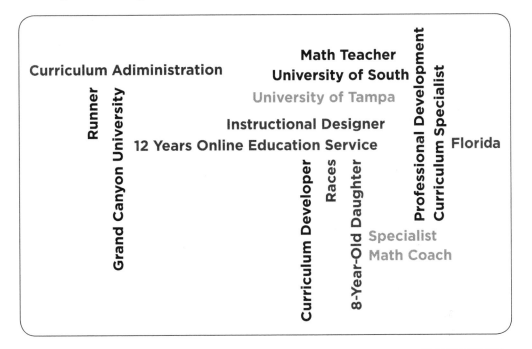

Figure 4.6: Sample word collage that highlights the facilitator's background.

- **Discussion icebreaker:** You can implement this icebreaker live or through an asynchronous platform (such as VoiceThread). Ask students to post information about their lives (such as what they do for fun or a hobby, information about their families, and so on), interest in the class subject matter (such as what they like about writing, solving mathematics problems, learning about history, and so on), and goals for the course (such as what they hope to learn or achieve by the end). You should also invite students to express any concerns they have about the course—ask questions like, "What is your biggest fear about writing?" "What is your biggest fear about giving presentations?" "Is there anything you are worried about regarding working on the topics in this class?" Ask probing questions to increase interactions among learners. For example, if a learner says he is not good in mathematics and is afraid of failing, ask the learner why he feels that way. Ask other learners to then share a time when they thought they might not do well in class (or other activity) and then did do well, and to relay what they did to succeed and learn the material.

- **Collaborative story icebreaker:** You can conduct this activity live or via a discussion thread. Start a story by creating a character based on yourself, and then ask learners to contribute to the story by adding characters and story lines based on their own lives. You might start off this icebreaker by stating, "Once upon a time, there was a woman who loved to tell stories. She also loved to teach students how to tell stories. She lived in a comfortable home with her husband and three children. Every day after waking up, she would put on her running shoes and go out for a thirty-minute run. She would then make breakfast for her family, and after sending them off to school, she would get on her computer to work with lots of other children, teaching them reading and writing skills. One day, when she went to her computer to work . . ." Learners can then piggyback on this story by adding their own background, interests, and so on. For example, one learner might say, "She found the computer would not turn on, and she got very upset."

- **Show-and-tell icebreaker:** This can be completed in a synchronous or asynchronous manner. Ask students to upload a photo of their favorite person, place, or thing. Ask the other students to comment on similarities or differences between what they posted and what others posted. Facilitators can also list all the items students have posted and ask them to vote on their favorite. If you employ this strategy in a synchronous classroom, begin this process as your students enter the classroom.

- **Team-building icebreaker:** When learners enter the course room, have them list their strengths (for example, *I am good at managing my time*, or *I am good at talking with other people*) and areas in which they feel they need assistance (*I am shy, and I don't like to present to other people*, or *I need examples to understand new concepts*). Then have them identify roles, based on their strengths, that they can assume when working on group tasks. Be sure to list some sample roles they might assume within their group (such as leader, recorder, task master, presenter, timekeeper, communication monitor, and so on), and then have them identify which role they would most like to take on when working with other learners. Encourage students to create additional titles and emphasize that everyone must assume a role.

- **Team capacity-building icebreaker:** Create a scenario in which each group needs to work to come to a consensus about how to solve a problem. The group presents their solution to the class. Other groups may then question and vote on the feasibility of the solution. For example, you might want to build team capacity but also teach an important concept such as how to be a good digital citizen and responsible digital learner. Therefore, you might ask learners to come up with a way to stop digital bullying and maintain good netiquette.

Using strategies like these to help build a sense of community among your students at the start of the course helps foster improved communication throughout the term as you engage them in a variety of lessons and challenges.

ERIC AND THE BLENDED LEARNING ENVIRONMENT

Eric is a social studies teacher at Liberty Middle School in Philadelphia, Pennsylvania. He had an exciting first day of school, greeting his students and asking each one of them to tell a one-minute story of his or her life. He consistently emphasizes that history is the telling of stories and he encourages students to reflect carefully on their past and use it as a mechanism for getting to know each other on the first day of school.

To extend this learning experience, he invited each participant to the class's digital collaborative learning space, to be used as a companion to his class throughout the year. For homework, he started an icebreaker collaborative story wherein he introduced a boy and a girl of middle school age who were living in Philadelphia in 1776. He playfully introduced the context to invite each student to add some details about the characters as part of a collaborative storytelling endeavor. As he logged into the platform he could see that his students were already eagerly at work, a benefit that carried over to the next day's classroom instruction as students discussed the story's progression.

We like these kinds of activities because, although 100 percent of virtual learning experiences will undoubtedly grow in popularity for certain students, the benefits of these blended learning experiences increase collaboration and represent the greatest area of potential growth in applying DEL. This icebreaker is a powerful one because it uses both face-to-face and online interaction between students to build a sense of community for the class.

Establish the Concept of Debate

Teaching students to learn to debate is a classic element of the instructional process. Researchers find that debate provides a means by which learners can actively engage in new learning and develop their critical-thinking and communication skills. Structured debate also provides a means by which critical dialogue can thrive (Jagger, 2013). In fact, research finds that debate increases student interest in subject matter thereby enhancing the potential that students come away with a better understanding of the material (Keller, Whitaker, & Burke, 2001; Vo & Morris, 2006). Therefore, incorporating structured debate and encouraging students to debate topics is an important part of the learning process. We recommend being very deliberate about teaching the concept of debate and making sure that learners understand that, in a virtual learning space, debate is a very powerful tool that allows for deep exploration of the content and improves engagement and understanding. To that end, here are some basic rules about how to lead a debate in a virtual learning space.

- Teach learners that it is perfectly acceptable to disagree with a classmate's position. Let learners know that they are always welcome to respectfully challenge and offer an alternative perspective regarding an *idea*. In the learning space, however, we do not debate *people*.

- When teaching debate, it is essential to remind students to avoid judgments. Don't leverage ideas as *good* or *bad*. Whenever possible, students should evaluate and measure concepts based on their merits.

- Make students aware that debate is a process in which those engaged in the debate must work diligently to hear the other person's message. Also, make sure they understand that they must seek to communicate in a way that clarifies their position. Emphasize that, whenever possible, students should back up the thoughts and positions they present in an online debate with facts and research.

- Emphasize that points of contention should never devolve into negativity or the use of a loud or an aggressive tone. In other words, emphasize that it is not permissible to type a message IN ALL CAPS. In virtual learning spaces, typing in all capital letters sends the message to the recipient that the speaker is shouting.

- When setting up debates and discussions, be thoughtful when grouping learners. Set up the learner experience with those who will conflict with each other but have commonalities between them. This allows them to reach resolution but engage in meaningful discussion.

- Give learners time and opportunities to reflect on their interactions with one another. Ask them to reflect on how they handled conflict or a given situation and think about how they may handle the situation differently in the future.

- When creating and facilitating discussion and debate, be sure to set expectations for interaction and model that behavior.
  - Be professional at all times.
  - Use humor sparingly and only if it is completely neutral.
  - Acknowledge conflicting points of view.
  - Offer research and sound arguments without emotional or personal opinion.
- Teach learners to give productive peer feedback, including sandwiching feedback to offer positives surrounding a conflicting point of view.
- Include team-building exercises in the initial part of the discussion or lesson so that learners do not see each other as strangers. Learners have a difficult time working with teammates they deem to be strangers (Keengwe et al., 2013).

Figure 4.7 is an example of a positive debate that follows these guidelines. If you give learners clear and explicit rules and a sense of safety within a positive learning culture, then debate can lead to a valuable learning experience.

Posted by Jennifer 08:02 a.m.

It does not matter if you vote. The popular vote versus the electoral votes are two different things. If you are in a state without a high number of electoral votes, you should not even bother. For example, I live in Rhode Island, with only four electoral votes. The state tends toward Democrat. If I am voting Republican, my one vote won't change Rhode Island's four electoral votes anyway.

Posted by Brian 08:32 a.m.

I hear and understand your position. Trust me when I say that every vote counts and every electoral vote counts. The four electoral votes in Rhode Island, for example, could be affected if enough people like you voted. And even if the state didn't change colors, it would be the beginning to a political climate change in the state, which could lead to a stronger popular vote in the election years to follow. That could eventually cause the state to have its four electoral votes go to Republicans. Your vote today could change everything.

Figure 4.7: Example of a positive debate.   CONTINUED →

> **Posted by Jennifer 08:34 a.m.**
>
> Thank you for your response, Brian. I do think you are right that if enough of us acted we could make a change. What about Florida? With twenty-nine electoral votes, how do my state's four votes matter?
>
> **Posted by Brian 08:53 a.m.**
>
> If you make a change in one state, and we all vote, making our own changes based on our political opinions, the climate of the political state of this whole country will change. We can make a difference.

When the debate is complete, you can help drive home the learning that occurs by encouraging, or even requiring, learners to keep a journal or engage in some other reflective process like writing one-minute papers, creating a photo collage, or drafting a digital story to convey and represent their ideas and new learning (Jehangir, 2012). Having students reflect on what they learn spurs additional ideas and innovations about the subject matter.

Conclusion

Many baseline assumptions or expectations for best practice associated with starting a face-to-face course are similarly applied when starting an online course. It is essential, however, that you keep in mind that the most important element of your digital learning facilitation is how well you establish and maintain dialogue threads. It is an important starting point, and you will see in the chapters that follow how essential it is to keep the course moving forward in an effective way. Chapter 5 deals with the issue of maintaining the momentum in the course after a strong start.

Maintaining the Momentum in the Learning Experience

So far in this book, you have had the opportunity to examine a best-practice overview on the philosophies and approaches to facilitating DEL. You have also explored strategies for setting up your digital learning experience and kicking off the experience in a way that is most likely to create high levels of engagement. The goal for the next three chapters is to identify strategies for maintaining the momentum, encouraging deeper levels of learning, and avoiding some significant challenges that could ultimately derail your progress.

KEY QUESTIONS ANSWERED IN THIS CHAPTER

- What are the strategies in facilitation that support engagement and growth in an online learning environment?

- How can you effectively apply each strategy for supporting engagement and growth in an online environment?

- How can you facilitate growth mindsets among all learners in the online classroom?

As you can tell from these key questions, the content that follows centers around establishing strategic practices that will help you maintain the strong start you established in your online course and encourage a deeper exploration of the learning you present. We refer to these strategies as *strategic facilitation*, a series of steps you can take as a facilitator that will have tremendous impact on your students. From there, we talk about the importance of helping your students maintain growth mindsets.

Digitally Enhanced Learning and Strategic Facilitation

For all the complexity inherent in engaging students in learning online, we've boiled down the most critical aspects into twelve core suggestions for strategic facilitation. We designed these strategies to maximize engagement and create dynamic learning opportunities for your students.

Maintain an Ongoing Presence

As we recommended in the previous chapter, it is important that the learners see evidence of facilitator presence. The presence of your comments throughout the digital environment sends the message that, as a facilitator, you are aware of what is going on in the class and are vigilant in terms of reviewing and addressing student posts, questions, and observations. It is extremely helpful to get into the course either every day or at least six days a week. This creates a sense of security for learners, knowing that you are there and are aware of each student's activity. It also helps reduce bullying and other off-task behavior. Your ongoing presence supports their free-flowing participation.

Monitor Commentary Length

Although a teachable moment may erupt in which you feel the need to elaborate rather thoroughly in a discussion board or by posting an announcement regarding something you have observed, keep in mind that if your commentary is too long, students simply won't read it. Think about emails you have received in the past from friends or colleagues that were extraordinarily long. In many cases, your first inclination was to ignore the commentary altogether. The appropriateness of commentary length is driven to some degree by the developmental level of your learners. It is also driven by the complexity of what you are attempting to communicate. The best way to relay complex content and a large amount of information is to break them down into chunks (Fonollosa, Neftci, & Rabinovich, 2015; Watson, Wirtz, & Sumpter, 2015). Therefore, consider using headings, colored text, photos, illustrations, and clear and concise verbiage to convey your intended message (see figure 5.1).

Make New Community Connections

In addition to chunking your content, establishing new connections with your student community helps keep learners engaged. When it comes to learning, novelty is extraordinarily powerful. When novelty is introduced, our brains tend to devote more power and attention to that new element. Thus, we tend to hang on to that new learning with greater fidelity (Lee, O'Doherty, & Shimojo, 2015).

Greetings Class,

I can see that many of you are struggling a bit with solving a problem in the right order using PEMDAS (**P**arentheses, **E**xponents, **M**ultiplication and **D**ivision, **A**ddition and **S**ubtraction).

Let's take a problem such as $8 + (2 \times 3^2 - 8 \div 2)$

First, you need to solve what's in the parenthesis.

$(2 \times 3^2 - 8 \div 2)$

In order to do this, solve the exponent, which equals 2 times 9, or (3^2), minus 8 divided by 2.

Then, solve the multiplication and division (the order doesn't matter with that).

$2 \times 9 = 18$

$8 \div 2 = 4$

Then , add or subtract what is in the parenthesis (in this case, you will subtract).

$18 - 4 = 14$

Then, you add or subtract what is outside of the parenthesis (in this case, you will add).

So $8 + 14 = 22$

The answer is 22.

Now try this problem, and explain each step of the process (as I did above) that you completed to get your answer: $7 - (6 \times 2^2 - 7 \div 2)$

Figure 5.1: Example of a way to limit commentary length.

One way to keep momentum going in your course is to invite a guest speaker, either synchronously (in the form of a webinar or such) or asynchronously (in the form of a preestablished interview or commentary posted online). Think about how much novelty is introduced with this simple action. In this context, learners have an opportunity to experience the outside input of a guest speaker by simply reading the narrative interview. They also have an opportunity to directly interact with the guest speaker as they log in and participate in the conversation (see figure 5.2, page 82).

Hello Class! I know that I have told you many times about my interesting college roommate, Kelly Horn. We were in many classes together in college, although her major was zoology. Today she works at the Bronx Zoo. Interestingly, she oversees their reptile house! Since we are studying reptiles, I interviewed her about some of the animals she cares for and some of their habits that she has observed. Below, click on the audio link that contains our interview. After listening to the interview, post some questions in the discussion log. Kelly has agreed to log in and provide you with answers to whatever questions might come up for you. This is due on Wednesday. Thank you very much!

Figure 5.2: Example of engaging students by bringing in an outside speaker.

Also consider having learners connect digitally with expert bloggers or professional Twitter forums to establish ongoing dialogues regarding important course topics. These forums can help them establish ongoing and meaningful connections with experts on the respective subject matter, gain insights, and even engage in discussions to enhance their knowledge around the subject matter.

Offering assignments that connect learners with their local community, called *service learning*, is another way to engage students. For example, a lesson on the environment is a grand opportunity for students to get involved in their community recycling program and apply their classroom content to real-world solutions. To accomplish this, with safety in mind, review your organizational policies around student interaction in community groups, connect with parents and students as to what group they have chosen, and ensure that parents agree to the assignment. Your organization will likely require that parents and students sign a safety agreement for the student to engage in a community activity for a grade.

Ask Strategic, Meaningful Questions

One of the most powerful forces in learning is inquiry. Many learning theorists believe that our evolution as a species and ability to innovate are driven to a great extent by our capacity to identify seminal questions and pursue answers and resolutions (Vadeboncoeur, Alkouatli, & Amini, 2015). As a result, asking questions in a virtual learning experience keeps the momentum going and helps ensure that the learning experience remains dynamic and demands a degree of interaction (Wu, Tseng, & Hwang, 2015).

Although it is our position that inquiry works in almost any learning environment, it's especially effective in online learning spaces. The reason it works so well is because when we collaborate in a digital learning space we often lack personal context and the ability to read each other in the moment. In some learning environments, if dialogue isn't encouraged, participants are sometimes a bit nervous about jumping in and posting a thought or a comment. Put another way, if you are at a party you might observe the body language of other partygoers, including facial expressions, hand gestures, and just the general warmth of the room. This helps create a context where it is more likely that you will speak up and begin to dialogue with fellow guests. In digital learning spaces this is a little more difficult to create. Therefore, friendly questions create an opportunity for rich and dynamic interactions.

It is not unrealistic to pose a question in an online learning space and require every learner to respond; interactions that often aren't possible with synchronous face-to-face meetings. Consider an example in which you ask students to flip a coin twice and determine the probability of getting two heads. As students post their answers to the whiteboard, you can follow up as in figure 5.3.

Johnny, I see that you solved this by using a tree diagram, and George, you used the conditional probability formula. Can you each explain your reasoning?

Choose one or two people who solved this differently than you and go into a breakout room together. Please come back and respond to the following.

1. After reviewing each other's methods, decide which is the best method.

2. Which one gives you the answer the fastest? Explain the mathematical reasoning behind the method.

3. Did one of you get it wrong? Explain how and why the method failed to result in the correct answer.

Figure 5.3: Sample questions to inspire teamwork and inquiry.

This kind of follow-up, using questions to bring students together, fosters ongoing engagement in the learning.

Continue to Personalize and Humanize the Digital Environment

We recommended in chapter 3 that facilitators post a biography, a friendly picture, and even a video introduction and content overview. We believe this is a helpful step in situations where the students and the facilitator never meet or are enjoying a blended learning experience with both face-to-face and virtual experiences. To keep the momentum going, however, we believe it is helpful to occasionally post some additional video commentary from the facilitator.

In face-to-face learning experiences, learners undoubtedly get to know their teachers or professors as they spend more time working together. The same should be true in a virtual learning environment. In addition to sharing a bit more information about yourself and bringing your own tone and personality to your work, using video, or even just audio, adds much-needed personalization that doesn't come through in text communication. Simple, short, virtual interactions, where the learners can see their instructor, are powerful. If you try this with your course, however, keep in mind the accessibility requirements of all your students. If necessary, create a text version of your video or audio for learners with visual or hearing impairments using tools to read the text on screen.

You can use these elements as often as you like; however, be mindful of differentiating the types of resources your offer to the class so that students stay engaged. Consider using this sort of media in timed durations, such as weekly, and solicit feedback from your students as to their benefit and drawbacks. In addition to sharing more as a facilitator, look for opportunities to learn more about your students. Students often open up to genuine human connections in digital environments. That connection can lead to greater engagement, and greater engagement generates deep learning!

Post Engaging Challenges or Problems to Solve

Introducing a fun and interesting challenge can keep the learners engaged and may give them some fun and unique ways to apply their learning. Consider the example in figure 5.4.

Survivor: The Two-Thousand Calorie Challenge

As you know, we have been studying food, nutrients, and caloric intake over the last week and a half. For this discussion, imagine we have been invited to participate in the TV show *Survivor*. As guests on the show, you will be sent to a rugged and remote island in the Pacific. The show is calling this episode "The Two-Thousand Calorie Challenge." This is because you must create a two-thousand calorie diet with the food you are provided. Keep this in mind:

1. Your diet can consist of any combination of food choices you would like.

2. Your diet should be designed to maintain high levels of energy due to the physical challenges you will face on the island.

Attached to this assignment, find the rubric we have been using to identify the differences between a healthy and an unhealthy diet. In making these selections, also try to pick foods you would like to eat.

Figure 5.4: Example of a fun and unique challenge.

This *Survivor* challenge is fun for a couple of reasons. First, students can relate to a popular television show and, by participating in this learning experience, they can imagine themselves as reality television stars, and not just middle school students. Second, it's very specific and requires the collaboration of a few learning variables that force the learners to integrate several outcomes at once. Obviously, this is the case in any type of activity wherein we ask students to collaborate and solve a problem. At a distance, however, students can also build colingual relationships with one another and develop those relationships into deeper connections.

Introduce Digital Bell Ringers

Many of the best face-to-face instructors know that a bell-ringer activity—an activity you introduce at the very beginning of class—is one step you can take to facilitate a strong start to your instruction. While popular in physical classrooms, bell-ringer activities, like the one featured in figure 5.5, are possible in a virtual learning space as well.

As we begin our unit on the U.S. voting process, we are going to start by examining the Electoral College. First write down what you know about the Electoral College. Then review information at www.history.com/topics /electoral-college about the Electoral College.

Share two things you learned about the Electoral College that you did not know before reviewing the site about the Electoral College.

Figure 5.5: Example of a bell-ringer activity.

Bell ringers are helpful because students enter the class and begin working immediately, which helps students put themselves on task. These short, fun assignments prepare a cognitive bridge from the introductory activity to the assignment for the day.

Revisit Learning Goals

We talked in chapter 4 about the importance of establishing specific learning goals for every student. In some cases, you may elect to establish learning goals for a team of students working together, as well as learning goals for the entire class. Whenever possible, as a mechanism for keeping the learning going in the class, strategically review those learning goals as the course progresses (see figure 5.6).

Learning goal: Understand the real-world applications of right triangle trigonometry.

Have you ever driven across the Golden Gate Bridge? You could not have done so without using knowledge like what you'll use in this chapter!

Let's revisit right triangle trigonometry and determine how this bridge stays up! **The Golden Gate Bridge facts:**

- 8,981 feet long

- 746 feet tall

- 220 feet in elevation

Be the engineer: To keep people safe on this magnificent bridge, engineers must use exactly what you learned here. Assuming the base of the bridge must be equidistant on both sides to the middle point of the bridge, use your right triangle trigonometry to determine the exact distance in feet from the base of one side of the middle of the bridge at the highest point. Be sure! If you make a mistake, the bridge could come tumbling down.

Figure 5.6: Example of revisiting a learning goal.

This example is powerful because it allows the teacher to revisit the learning goals by using an activity that is realistically applied. Most students have at least seen a picture of this bridge and can imagine the provided challenge. Not unlike the previous *Survivor* example, it puts them to work thinking about what could be a real-life problem and it makes the learning fun, applied, and more interesting.

Release More Resources

In chapter 3, we discussed the importance of not posting too much information all at once. Holding back some resources that you can introduce at strategic points later in the course helps maintain learner engagement and avoids overwhelming the students with too much information in too short a time. Posting a new video, sharing a new article, or identifying a helpful link as a new resource, once again, creates a sense of engagement and novelty.

Post Engaging Multimedia Interjections

In addition to maintaining a gradual release of strategic resources, it is helpful to interject engaging multimedia. This is a bit different from recording your own audio or video as a way of being more personal with your students. With this sort of media we're talking about outside learning sources that go beyond more assigned reading on the Internet. This video is best interjected in a review of a module or semester. To illustrate, the example in figure 5.7 helps students draw from multiple physics concepts they studied in their course to form new connections with the subject matter.

Insert: A video of mountain bikers riding on a mountaintop jumping crevices and cliffs

Ask students: "What observations do you make about their calculated moves? How does this relate to physics? What would the biker need to know about physics to help him or her successfully finish this challenging ride? Remember to research and organize your thoughts with sources."

Figure 5.7: Example of an engaging multimedia interjection.

Sharing sources that come from multiple types of media engages students and maintains momentum. If you happen to know of powerful video clips that demonstrate unique aspects of the course, a strategic and thoughtfully timed infusion of these videos can make a big difference.

Use Humor Carefully

It's true that the best teachers use humor effectively. With an eye on maintaining momentum, humor helps connect people to the learning experience. As a teacher, you don't have to be a comedian. Do not forget that humor does not always translate as intended a virtual learning experience. For example, certain face-to-face cues that help inject humor into a message are not available in a virtual learning space. In a digital environment, a bit of self-deprecating humor, without an attached smile or the appropriate intonation, may instead be interpreted as sarcasm or worse. With that said, we still believe humor is important. For example, a funny assignment, like the one in figure 5.8, may be a great opportunity for humor.

Benjamin Franklin Is Grounded Again

Over the past several weeks, you've learned a lot about the life and times and contributions of Benjamin Franklin. Your innovation paper will be driven by insights about Franklin's ability to see the world differently and create. Based on what we've learned about Benjamin Franklin, I'd like you to think about what he would be like if he were an eighth-grade boy living in your neighborhood. For this discussion question, I'd like you to imagine that your friend, Ben, has gotten in trouble at home and has been grounded for a month! In a minimum of three-hundred words, I'd like you to explain what you think Ben would have done that would have resulted in his parents grounding him. Think about his own creative approaches to problem solving and then imagine what might have gotten him into trouble at home. Describe what he might have done and what you think he might say to his parents to get out of trouble. Make sure that you are very specific in your references to what you know about Benjamin Franklin in your example.

Figure 5.8: Example of using humor effectively.

Showing the students your willingness to have fun—that learning is fun—can help them engage with online learning instead of becoming bored with it. That outcome is worth a calculated risk.

Take Advantage of the Power of Celebration and Engagement

Whether you work in an online or a physical classroom, celebration and encouragement are some of the most powerful tools you can use. In online learning spaces, however, there are some distinctions. When providing praise in this space, use a wide variety of specific comments as you communicate with your students. For example, if you overuse a generic phrase, such as "good job," students will begin to see it as meaningless or benign. When you provide encouragement or celebrate accomplishments, you can make that positive feedback more powerful and meaningful by being explicit and specific. When complimenting an answer, for example, being able to draw learners' attention back to a specific thing they learned in relationship to a preestablished rubric or learning expectation makes your compliment far more authentic. In so doing, you might consider writing a personal note to a learner commending his or her work (see figure 5.9).

Hi Tom,

I wanted to send you a note letting you know that I am very impressed with your ability to create an attention-getter that not only captures the readers' attention but also clearly represents and illustrates exactly what you cover in your paper. Writing a clear and captivating attention-getter is no small feat, but you have obviously mastered the challenge. Good work!

Mr. Jones

Figure 5.9: Sample personal note celebrating a student's work.

You might also consider creating a collage of your class's best work in the form of a video clip that highlights outstanding work from multiple students on a project. You might even create a bulletin board in your digital classroom that you update each week with displays of the best work your learners submit.

Growth Mindsets in Online Learning

In the previous section, we articulated twelve steps you can take to maintain strategic facilitation of your digital environment. Undergirding these suggestions for maintaining the momentum in a digital environment is the all-important priority of establishing and maintaining a growth mindset. In this section, we define and illustrate a growth mindset which, we suggest, is altogether necessary to avoid the debilitating impacts of a fixed mindset. Understanding individual student mindsets is critical to all teaching practices, online or offline, but online-only classrooms, in particular, require you to alter how you assess and engage your students according to their respective mindsets.

Students with *growth mindsets* believe that they can overcome challenges and have the capacity to build knowledge and skill sets. Students with *fixed mindsets* believe that they have certain innate talents and skills that can be nurtured but that their limitations cannot be changed or improved on, such as *I'm just not good at mathematics* (Dweck, 2015). Students who have fixed mindsets are obsessed with the possibility of making mistakes and have serious doubts about their ability to successfully perform tasks. These students often give up and too often are deemed as lazy. On the contrary, these students are not lazy; they just don't believe that they have the capability of completing the tasks or assignments, so they decide that it's not worth their time to even try. These are the students who don't turn in work or consistently turn in work that is incomplete or does not meet standard. They are afraid to ask questions because they don't want to look dumb, incompetent, or stupid. They don't believe they can achieve in a given area and, therefore, are less willing to put forth the effort to try because they are convinced doing so is a waste of time and they will fail anyway (Flett & Hewitt, 2014).

Students with growth mindsets are more resilient toward challenges and are not worried about looking dumb; they will continue to work toward learning more and doing better. Studies show that learners with strong growth mindsets are not as apt to experience performance angst or be affected by stereotypes, and it is more likely that they will not obsess over mistakes but will learn from them. In other words, motivation and cognitive ability, performance, and growth are interrelated and are not separate entities (Sparks, 2015). The objective of individuals with fixed mindsets is to appear smart, and the goal of individuals with growth mindsets is to work to become smarter (Jacobson, 2013).

Because students with fixed mindsets obsess over how their teacher and peers will perceive their work and performance, they see setbacks as an indication of their limited talents (Dweck, 2015). These students often disregard helpful feedback and feel threatened by others' success (Dweck, 2010). They're so afraid of failing that they may even cheat because they are afraid they will be wrong (Jacobson, 2013).

Research shows that what a learner believes about him- or herself to be true (despite any data that suggest differently) affects his or her motivation to try to learn. Students who have fixed mindsets depend on their teachers for all the answers and do not assume ownership over their own learning (Sparks, 2015). Therefore, to create and maintain momentum in a digital classroom, facilitators must help students with fixed mindsets develop growth mindsets and help learners with growth mindsets maintain and nurture those mindsets.

To help students develop growth mindsets, it is important to avoid overreacting to or admonishing learners for late work or work that is incorrect. Doing so gives fixed-mindset learners the impression that they are unable to get work done correctly or on time. Approaching learners who turn in work late by asking them how to solve the issue and providing suggestions for doing so goes a long way in empowering them to adopt growth mindsets and feel that submitting work is within their power.

In addition, working with students who make mistakes in their work and helping them find ways to fix those issues shows them that they are capable of growth and development and that the learning process is iterative and ongoing. For example, in looking over a student's work, you might find that he misread the directions. By offering feedback that directs him to reread the directions and alter the work accordingly, you are showing him that mistakes are fixable, and it is within his power to fix them. You are also showing him that the focus is on learning growth and not on getting something right the first time, every time. Helping learners see their mistakes as opportunities for growth and improvement facilitates the development of growth mindsets. Helping them see that mistakes are fixable, and guiding them in problem solving to fix mistakes and overcome challenges, facilitates mindsets wherein they see learning as a continuous process, not a one-shot endeavor (Flett & Hewitt, 2014). Consider the following strategies.

- **Use praise only to affirm valued qualities:** Cooperation, critical thinking, problem solving, persistence, analysis, and so on—these are all on the spectrum of valued student qualities in any classroom. When students fail to exhibit these qualities in some way, always provide suggestions and redirection to put them back on the right path. We shouldn't simply say "good effort." We need to only affirm good effort if it is aligned with the goals and objectives of the task, assignment, or initiative and the values we want to uphold. Use constructive feedback that requires student follow-up, such as, "Good, now keep chipping away at that answer." "What needs to be done first in order to solve the problem?" "Let's work to uncover a solution." "Let's try again to see if we can come up with something else; another idea or a solution." This sort of feedback encourages students to keep trying and view learning as a continuous process (Sullivan, 2011).

- **Teach students how to find answers and information:** Students with fixed mindsets constantly worry that they are going to look stupid or dumb because they believe that there is not much (if anything) they can do about their ability to learn a new concept or skill. Therefore, it is important to create an environment in which students are encouraged to search for answers to inquiries and wherein you embrace all questions as valid and valued—patience is key. Help students focus on how to find answers and develop procedures for finding information instead of focusing on whether answers are right or wrong. For example, "This may not be accurate. How do you find more accurate information to inform your inquiry?"

- **Avoid demanding that there is only one right way to accomplish a task:** Encourage students to explore and experiment with multiple strategies and ways for completing work, tasks, and such. Allow students to try a myriad of strategies for solving mathematics equations beyond what you have instructed them to do.

- **Give assignments that promote inquiry, not memorization:** Avoid emphasis on right or wrong answers. If students in a blended classroom are expected to know something and you are giving a test on the material, allow them to use their notes to take the test. Very few people are good at memorizing large amounts of information, and even fewer are good at retaining memorized information in their long-term memory. Focus on learning the material and then test for learning growth instead of memory.

- **Develop a rating category for self-assessment of effort:** If a student comes to you and says he can't find information about a topic he is asked to research, ask, "On a scale of one to ten, how hard have you tried to find information?" If the student says, "Three," then ask more questions to determine what he needs to do to continue looking for an answer. You might even provide a few suggestions on where he might look or search terms he might use to find information. This can encourage students to continue to put effort into their tasks, assignments, and inquiry pursuits (Jacobson, 2013).

- **Check your own mindset:** Do you expect students to already know what you convey in your class? Do you see students as lazy or incapable? If the answer to these questions is yes, then consider changing your mindset to one by which you believe that all students are capable of learning and growing.

- **Encourage risk taking and discomfort in the learning process:** There is tremendous value in learning from error. Intelligence in any area is built by working "through the initial discomfort of situations that don't make sense" (Miller, 2013, p. 61). In other words, intelligence is built through trial and error and the capacity to perceive challenges or difficulties as opportunities to pause, review, and implement protocols for understanding and figuring out problems (Newkirk, 2012). Another factor to consider is that doubt, while annoying and uncomfortable, "prompts inquiry or investigation" (Miller, 2013, p. 62). The mind, much like a muscle, strengthens when you use it.

- **Model the growth mindset for learners:** Show students how to work to solve problems by demonstrating your own ability to solve problems, admit mistakes, and discuss strategies for fixing them or overcoming challenges.

- **Set up students to win:** Give students work on the subject matter that they can easily master and then scaffold instruction and practice in a way that enables them to continuously build their knowledge and skills, gradually increasing the challenge level of the work. Provide guided practice and empowering feedback. Offer suggestions instead of critical feedback. Provide students with examples of others who struggled but overcame challenge and adversity to succeed. To help learners develop growth mindsets, feedback, encouragement, and praise must be specific and support oriented. For example, simply encouraging learners to keep working or to work harder to improve may not be accurate or good enough. We have to assess the degree to which learners have the necessary foundational skills, are employing the right strategies, and are being supported and guided in their effort before we simply say, "Keep working." We have to assess what they need to improve in a given area—learners can only achieve if they have the right tools and are using the right strategies. Developing growth mindsets entails taking a realistic look at what learners need in order to accomplish learning goals (Dweck, 2015).

- **Avoid placing emphasis on speed in providing answers or completing tasks:** Students come into the class with a variety of cognitive processing capacities. Some students' brains process information rapidly, while others need more time. Although asynchronous online platforms mitigate this problem, you should take this into consideration when facilitating in a synchronous classroom. Overemphasis on speed creates a lot of anxiety in students who process information at slower speeds.

- **Avoid focusing on the small stuff:** It is important to avoid focusing on the little details like spelling or sloppy presentation and instead focus on the substance of the content students present, as well as the goals for the assignment, lesson, task, or assessment. Focus on whether or not the learner is processing the information and if he or she is able to do the skill in question. Then provide suggestions for improvement, rather than a critical analysis of what went wrong. If learners become overwhelmed by too many little issues, they will disengage from the learning process. Focus on the big ideas relative to the goals and objectives of the lesson.

Use of these strategies will help your fixed-mindset students alter their thinking toward growth mindsets, something that will help them succeed not only in your online classroom, but in future classrooms and life.

Conclusion

This chapter explored several strategies you can utilize as a facilitator to keep the momentum going in your class. Although some may appear more managerial than you might like, these suggestions ultimately have an impact on the class culture and climate. If you employ all or most of these suggestions, we are confident your online learning experience will continue to excite the students you serve throughout the term of the curriculum.

CHAPTER 6

Teaching Thoughtful Online Collaboration

In this chapter, we continue our conversation regarding the steps that best-practice facilitators of DEL take to keep the positive momentum going. In chapter 5, we talked about some thoughtful strategies that, if implemented, will help you maintain higher levels of engagement. In this chapter, we address arguably the most important element of all in terms of positive momentum: maintaining a culture and climate of thoughtful conversation and collaboration. With almost two decades of experience, we have come to the conclusion that the most important learning experience revolves around the interactions students are able to enjoy with their facilitator and classmates. The degree to which an online learning experience offers safe and thoughtful opportunities for this kind of discourse often drives the success of the experience. Suffice it to say, this is an important chapter.

KEY QUESTIONS ANSWERED IN THIS CHAPTER

- What steps can you take to ensure thoughtful, respectful, learning-centered, and engaging virtual collaborations and conversations?
- How do teams impact online learning environments?
- How do collaboration requirements impact online learning environments?

Let us look at some of the advantages individual learners, not to mention the whole class, will realize as a result of committing to deep, ongoing, thoughtful collaboration in a digital learning environment.

Goals and Commitments

In this section we outline some of the advantages in store for learners when facilitators of DEL make a commitment to facilitating thoughtful conversations and deep collaboration in digital learning environments.

Improved Writing

One advantage of establishing a system of thoughtful, ongoing virtual dialogue is that it offers the opportunity to improve the writing capacity of everyone in the course (Alvarez, Espasa, & Guasch, 2012). We recommend facilitators maintain high expectations regarding writing proficiency in the virtual learning environment. Although you always want to remember whether students have growth or fixed mindsets, there are standards you need them to strive to meet. It is a mistake, for example, to allow students to use texting-style communication shortcuts. This is a place to practice and celebrate writing and the ability to enhance communication in all subject areas.

At the most practical and obvious levels it is clear to see that, in an environment where all or most collaboration is done cyber-asynchronously, skill sets around writing and language development must be enhanced to meet these emerging expectations. If you break a leg, your arms usually get stronger because you depend on them more to get you around. If you cannot rely on a smile, a nod, or any other form of physical communication, then your writing is forced to communicate for you, which will develop your writing skills.

Equalization of Student Voice

In DEL spaces, give students equal opportunity to contribute to discussions. Those louder and more aggressive students who tend to dominate face-to-face, synchronous social environments do not have the same advantage in a virtual learning space. This is not to imply that verbose conversation domination can't occur in a digital learning environment, but the fact that there is equity in terms of the tools the speakers use represents a unique advantage. To be even more specific, a thoughtful and quiet student may feel social and some form of undergirded physical intimidation if a loud, dominating classmate talks over them. In a conversation thread in a digital classroom that same student may feel frustrated by an avalanche of verbal rebuttals in text form, but they won't necessarily feel the social or physical intimidation. Many DEL facilitators report this to be beneficial because they can discover untapped potential in those students who may not normally contribute in other environments.

Opportunity to Hear From Each Student

In most face-to-face classroom conversations, teachers do not have the opportunity to call on every student every day. However, because of the convenience and reach of online learning, facilitators have the opportunity to connect more consistently with every student (Lawes, 2015). This provides academic advantages as well, because teachers can more comprehensively and formatively assess student progress through phone calls, written feedback, and collaborative environments. It also provides several social advantages, given the opportunity to connect and check in on students' relative well-being (Vonderwell & Boboc, 2013). For example, if Lisa is teaching a cyber-asynchronous learning experience, she can easily ask students to check in with her on Wednesday, articulate in one sentence their reflections on the readings that week, and ask any questions they may have. She can then quickly scan those replies and provide personalized responses to each learner while she assesses his or her understanding. Or, she could pursue this in a subtler way by evaluating student engagement each week and then reaching out to individual students she hasn't heard from as a mechanism for ensuring that every student is involved.

Continued Evaluation and Understanding

As students work in a DEL space, they leave breadcrumbs of evidence for the instructor as to their relative progress and understanding. A teacher can gain valuable insights by evaluating a student's work, reading an original post, participating in a discussion thread, and following up on student questions. The good news for facilitators is that these virtual breadcrumbs are left hanging in abeyance in the classroom, allowing the instructor to revisit these data points for continuing student evaluation and understanding. This is contrary to the idea face-to-face instructors sometimes pose that virtual learning spaces often cause us to overlook valuable information about the student. Although physical observations may not be available, students provide us much information throughout these exchanges. Not only that, but you can go back and review online work and behavior as often as you need to, whereas a live interaction is subject to the vagaries of human memory.

Thoughtful, Respectful, Rule-Bound Discussion and Debate

To maintain momentum in an online learning experience, facilitators must make a direct and public commitment to maintaining a safe and respectful environment that is also challenging and thought provoking (Lee, Pate, & Cozart, 2015). Undergirding this idea is the notion that we are advantaged in the learning process when we create a bit of dissonance. Anybody reading this book has undoubtedly had a professor who, at some point, made a habit of confronting students with strongly held beliefs as a way of challenging them to be more thoughtful in their presentation, consider alternate perspectives, or even reconsider their facts.

This notion of disciplined examination of other perspectives is extraordinarily valuable as our world becomes increasingly diverse and technology allows us to consistently do businesses with people who live lives very different than our own. To that end, teachers working in virtually any type of learning environment need to teach discussion and debate in a more formalized and disciplined way. Once again, we see the ability to teach this invaluable skill enhanced when working in a DEL environment. We discuss some of the necessary rules later in this chapter (see page 100).

Collaboration and Teaming

Although teaming is not necessarily an integral aspect of every well-facilitated online learning experience, we wholeheartedly recommend it as a best-practice approach. Simply put, teaming works. It is especially helpful in the virtual context because it gives teachers another opportunity for the students to feel connected to the learning experience (Park & Seo, 2013). Remember, when students are working online, they may sometimes feel isolated. Assigning a student to a team is a means to ensure that students recognize relationships with teachers, team members, and classmates.

KIAH AND THE GROUP ASSIGNMENT

Kiah is a ninth-grade student taking a civics class in a digital learning environment. The class is debating issues on the topic of search and seizure on school property. The instructor puts the students in teams and asks them to work together to devise an assigned position on the topic. They weren't given the choice to pick a side regarding the topic. Instead the teacher assigned a position and they had to develop an argument or case for that position. They then collectively posted their position in the digital learning environment. Other teams then purposefully deconstructed each argument and offered a rebuttal. Later, the instructor asks Kiah to work with his same team in constructing an equally well-prepared argument supporting a different position on the topic.

By establishing these parameters, consider the volume of thinking this required of students. The students were asked to defend what might be their natural position as well as defend a position that they don't necessarily champion. They had to rebut their own opinions. Perhaps most challenging of all is the fact that they had to commit all of this to writing. Kiah and his classmates may have been emotionally bursting at the seams about a topic; however, instead of shouting or gesticulating, they had to come up with a thoughtful way to construct their sentences and paragraphs to make their case. Furthermore, they worked together in a team to come up with a compelling argument or rebuttal. Each step along the way required thoughtful collaboration and consideration of their perspective as well as others' perspectives.

As the example of Kiah demonstrates, online teams have unique advantages, so let us examine some of the strategic steps facilitators can take to help make them work. When you utilize teams in your online learning space, the students may tell you they prefer to work alone. Share the following advantages with them, help them engage their growth mindsets, and give teamwork a chance.

- **Teaming and brain stimulation:** Remind reluctant students of the fact that some of the deepest levels of neurological engagement are generated when a diverse group of colleagues work together (Holzweiss, Joyner, Fuller, Henderson, & Young, 2014). This has been proven many times via brain science experiments, and researchers have discovered greater left and right brain hemispheric connectivity when learners are asked to experience the learning process as part of a diverse team of peers (Woolley et al., 2007).

- **Teaming and the world of work:** Yet another rationale to share with students who may be resistant to the teaming process is the notion of teaming in the 21st century workplace. It is non-negotiable in many work environments, and often evaluations are conducted both individually and in relationship to team performance. Present the future economic implications of teamwork as yet another rationale to virtual learning students (Witteveen, 2015).

- **Teaming and high expectations (learning and social):** Finally, teaming offers the opportunity to create conditions for additional reinforcement in learning and social expectations. For example, if the facilitator shares a particular learning goal to be achieved by a certain time, the focus of the group will help make that deadline real and hopefully motivate participants to adhere to expected time lines and focus on the learning ahead. Furthermore, as the facilitator provides social and behavioral expectations, teams are again helpful in providing observation and accountability (Holzweiss et al., 2014). Teammates can often remind one another of the expectations for their work.

Choosing how to distribute students among teams can feel like a difficult task, especially if you have students who struggle when asked to work as a group. There are several ways to facilitate team creation that engage your students and get the best work from them.

- **Random selection:** We think that, when choosing teams that must work together for an extended period, random selection may not be the best idea. The wrong mix of learners may significantly influence a learning team in a negative way. However, by occasionally having random teams assigned, and studying the work outputs, you may find that students perform unexpectedly well under certain circumstances. For whatever reason, a certain alchemy of factors of a randomly assigned team may bring out some skills that even your own strategic efforts wouldn't have yielded. Sometimes leaving it to chance allows you to study unexpected results.

- **Student choice:** Allowing students the opportunity to pick their own teams also provides advantages for enhanced online collaboration. This may not work as well in a blended classroom, where students may know each other very well, but if students arrive in the online learning class not knowing each other, they must take the initiative to get to know one another well enough to make up the teams. In observance of these virtual conversations, the facilitator can begin to ascertain personality types and other details that may guide future facilitation. Experimenting with a student-led team, even if they are together for just a short time, allows you to better ascertain who your class leaders may be. It also may help you identify students who may be ready to lead with some encouragement.

- **Facilitator created:** This strategy allows facilitators to be strategic and put together more diverse teams in terms of background, experience, and perhaps even capacity. More heterogeneous teams tend to outperform more homogeneous teams in both face-to-face and online settings. Thus, we recommend striving for diversity in your teams.

- **Size:** More research is needed regarding team size and associated learning benefits; however, there is some indication that a certain amount of social loafing (or free-rider effect) can take place in larger teams where some students fail to participate, either due to lack of confidence or because they believe the work counters their own benefit (Salomon & Globerson, 1989; Wang & Burton, 2010). If you find that happening, consider shrinking the team sizes you use in the future. With that rule of thumb in mind, we recommend that you form teams in digital environments under generally the same size permutations you would use in face-to-face, synchronous learning.

Whether you organize your students into teams or take a more directed, student-to-class approach, conversations will ensue.

Guidelines for Online Conversations and Collaboration

In this section, we provide basic guidance to help you train your students to collaborate and thoughtfully conduct online conversations that maximize their potential for growth.

Facilitator Input in Cyber-Asynchronous-Threaded Conversations

One of the most important decisions a facilitator must make is the degree to which he or she will contribute to conversations in learning spaces where dialogue is required. If a facilitator provides too much input, the dialogue suffers. The learner can experience cognitive overload and either ignore most of the message or discard it altogether. In our consulting practice, we call this the tennis match effect.

CRYSTAL AND THE TENNIS MATCH EFFECT

Crystal was teaching her first primarily cyber-asynchronous class. And she was excited! It was a U.S. History class being taught in a credit recovery school, and she was pleased to see that all twelve of her students have posted a response to an inquiry she made about the three factors that led up to World War I. Crystal is a morning person, so at 5 a.m. she began responding to each of her students. She saw that some of them posted as late as 11:30 p.m. the night before. For each student, she provided a one hundred fifty- to three hundred-word response with requests for follow-up.

The next morning, she noticed that many of her students had indeed responded. She was excited. The next day another discussion question she had posted was due, and once again she found that all twelve of her students responded. She also happily responded in kind with thoughtful facilitator responses. In her haste, she forgot to check for the requirement wherein students respond to one another. She posted a reminder and waited to see what would happen. To her disappointment, her students failed to provide much response to classmates. They met the required postings but the dialogue was uninspiring.

Crystal had experienced the tennis match effect. By the sheer velocity and volume of her answers, her students quickly got the message that this learning experience was all about maintaining an ongoing conversation with her. Even though she wanted students in her class to respond to one another, her reflections were far more thoughtful and complete than they could provide and it was easier for them to wait for her to provide an avalanche of dialogue and simply write her back.

The major disadvantage of the tennis match effect is that Crystal put herself in the position of coordinating an independent study for twelve students. Although her points were certainly good, and getting in and responding to students certainly added value to their insights into the content, in this case her enthusiasm may have intimidated the students and steered them away from engaging in conversations within the course room that could help them get to know the classmates and stimulate their thinking in a myriad of directions around the content. If a conversational tennis match takes place in your cyber-asynchronous class, try to be the umpire while students play the role of enthusiastic participants.

So, what could Crystal have done differently?

As she looked at discussion question number one and the responses, it would've been helpful for her to respond to a few and then ask several other students to respond to another student answer that was similar or quite different from their own. By doing this, Crystal reminds the participants that they should be observing what their classmates are saying. In some cases, students simply focus on what they are writing and what the instructor might think of what they write. By demanding consideration of other perspectives, you send the message that paying attention to other learners in the course room is essential. Ideally, facilitators should strive for rich and thoughtful conversations throughout the online classroom, strategically inserting thoughts, comments, and careful redirects en route to rich student-to-student dialogue and opportunities to reflect (Cheng, Pare, Collimore, & Joordens, 2011).

Respond to Thoughtful Student Posts

If you consider the example we just outlined, keep in mind two things. First, it's probably good to respond more at the beginning of the course. This shows that you're reading everything and, in some cases, a short acknowledgment of the post will keep the learning teams from feeling like you're dominating the conversation. Second, if you see the student has put a lot of time into a post, you might want to take the time to likewise respond in kind. For example, if one of Crystal's shy students wrote an unusually long post to a required reflection question, she should take the time to provide an equally thorough response to him or her as a way of recognizing that student's efforts and letting all students know that their words matter.

Learn to Respond Strategically

As you are reading this, you may feel a bit overwhelmed. We're giving you some examples wherein saying too much gets you in trouble and saying too little does the same. It is indeed a bit of an art, and you must be careful. In a face-to-face, synchronous class, you can make a sarcastic comment that perhaps is inconsistent with your ongoing interaction with your students and you can quickly vacate that comment with a myriad of affirmations, reinforcing it with facial and body language. However, a sarcastic comment from the instructor hangs in digital abeyance for all to see, perhaps reinforcing either the humiliation or simply the missed message. As a result, when facilitating cyber-synchronous conversations, facilitators must develop the capacity to provide strategic inputs so they can avoid the tennis match effect and likewise maximize learning potential.

When should you interject? Here are two examples.

1. **Little or no conversation:** If there is a lack of participation in a collaborative discussion space, the facilitator can begin the conversation and ask for student participation based on that input.

2. **Rants or disconnected thinking:** Although it is important to give students a chance to think and reflect, the virtual learning space should not become a bully pulpit for the ill-informed or the incorrect. If you notice critical errors or tangents in student reflection, it is important to provide the correct information or guidance back to the topic as soon as possible. In observing and facilitating learning online, look for unrelated commentary. Yes, you should permit some off-topic comments, but be sure to intervene and redirect students back to the topic at hand (Nandi et al., 2012).

In addition to strategically monitoring you own involvement in the discussion, there are multiple strategies you can deploy to promote rich discussion between students.

Strategies for Promoting Rich Discussion

When facilitating cyber-asynchronous learning experiences, our goal isn't just to avoid trouble or to minimize disruption. Indeed, if we do our jobs, students can engage in rich, thoughtful asynchronous discussions that can go on for days, include disagreements, become fortified with the inclusion of sources, get enhanced when others join the conversation, and generally benefit all participants individually and as a class. So, how do you get to these richer, more thoughtful discussions? Here is a list of eight strategies facilitators should employ to create rich discussion threads.

1. **Always make a connection first:** If students must share their thoughts in an online learning space, they need to trust in their connection with you. Icebreakers in the beginning of the course, like those we discussed in chapter 4, allow students to get to know you as well as each other.

2. **Respect privacy:** Students should know that their privacy, and that of their friends and collaborators, is respected. You must make it clear you will not make public any information they privately share without their consent.

3. **Establish respectful commentary lengths:** As we have stated, facilitators should be careful not to overwhelm students with feedback (Mazzolini & Maddison, 2007). In most cases, your response should be proportional to the length of the commentary. If a student writes a three-sentence post, a three hundred-word response would seem overwhelming. The inverse case is generally true as well.

4. **Encourage active levels of participation:** In a face-to-face classroom, facilitators must frequently encourage participation from students

who are less likely than others to speak in class. The same is true in many online learning endeavors. We encourage assignments for which everyone must participate and provide commentary, not only in relationship to the required assignment or prompt, but in relationship to each other as well (Nandi et al., 2012).

5. **Ask questions and seek clarification:** Inquiry is a powerful tool in improving conversations. When a student posts a statement, it may be helpful to ask questions to provide clarification or additional details, or perhaps ask another student his or her opinion of that post as a mechanism for creating new interactions (Curry & Cook, 2014; Nandi et al., 2012).

6. **Share a key resource:** In face-to-face learning opportunities, we often discuss teachable moments. Those teachable moments also emerge in asynchronous threaded discussions. Teachers observing the evolution of interesting dialogue might post a related resource, such as an article, a web link, or a video, as a mechanism for enhancing what is already in the dynamic conversation.

7. **Continue to follow the rules of debate:** In chapter 4, we discuss the value of debate and associated rules as a class activity. Many of these same rules apply in online discussion threads. Discourage declarations of right and wrong and encourage the presentation of thoughts and fearless defense of ideas.

8. **Have a goal:** When we ask students to collaborate, it is altogether essential to have a clear goal in mind. Just as a poorly facilitated face-to-face classroom discussion can veer off course and result in painful, off-task discussions, an asynchronous online discussion can do the same. For example, if Crystal posted a video about the Electoral College's role and provided rather nebulous directions regarding a discussion, she may check into her course one morning and find that students have participated in a fierce political debate that had little to do with the intended analysis of checks and balances. Her lack of a clear goal could lead to disruption, and, in this case, cause a political debate without context or direction. Always remember that clear goals for threaded virtual conversation enrich the conversation and maximize its potential to improve learning (Nandi et al., 2012).

As you employ these strategies, it is important to keep in mind your students' sophistication and capabilities. In many scenarios, students need to be taught how to have productive discussions.

Scaffolded Discussions

When engaging learners in collaborative discussions, scaffold and structure the discussion in a manner that facilitates gradual skill and concept building. Start off by asking questions that tap into comprehension, and then move into asking questions that prompt learners to connect what they already know to new concepts. From there, move to asking questions and assigning and facilitating tasks that get learners thinking about how they can use the concepts or skills in practical ways. Finally, always ask learners to reflect on what they learned, what they want to know more about, what they did well, and what they can improve (Mayes et al., 2011). Figure 6.1 demonstrates scaffolding in practice.

Comprehension: What did you learn about acids, bases, and neutrality by reading the chapter in your text and watching the assigned video? What are the dangers of using acidic substances?

Connection: What products do you use or consume that are considered acidic? What products do you use or consume that are considered a base? What products do you use or consume that are considered neutral substances?

Strategy and application: How are acids and bases used in everyday life? How do you use acids and bases in your life?

Reflection: What did you learn from this lesson that you can use in the future?

Figure 6.1: Example of scaffolding a chemistry lesson.

Scaffolding discussions, tasks, and assignments helps learners build on skills and gives them opportunities to practice and engage in the subject matter multiple times and in multiple ways.

Four Cs of Positive Online Discussion

Let's conclude this section with the four Cs of positive online discussion. These are camaraderie, confidence, cultures of trust, and capacity. Let us take a closer look at each one.

- **Camaraderie:** Camaraderie entails facilitating a course room climate in which participants feel a sense of pulling together to learn new content and practice new skills. Creating a sense of camaraderie requires facilitators to build in systems that prioritize interaction and encourage learners to build a sense of togetherness both in and beyond the online classroom. In other words, working to build lasting professional connections and friendships within the classroom systems helps learners feel more connected and motivated, and less isolated, alone, or fearful of engaging in the online learning community (Rogo & Portillo, 2015; Wei & Chen, 2012). Encourage learners to buddy up with a partner to edit each other's work and share ideas before formally presenting them. When students work together on important class projects, it can help enhance feelings of connection and togetherness. Instructors also play a role in the development of camaraderie by establishing a strong (but not stifling) online presence and offering timely and formative feedback along the way. If you follow the suggestions in this chapter and facilitate the learning experience with the goal of establishing and maintaining high levels of camaraderie, a better culture will emerge.

- **Confidence:** You must take steps to build the confidence of every learner you serve. Confidence, engagement, and learning growth are inextricably connected. Therefore, it is important to work to find every opportunity to build learner confidence (Howard & Whitaker, 2011; Wang, Shannon, & Ross, 2013). Creating opportunities for learners to demonstrate their expertise, knowledge, and growth in a topic area can serve to exponentially increase confidence. Send students an email or private note highlighting something specific they did (or said) to assist in increasing confidence and drive them toward growth mindsets. It is also helpful to make positive and affirming statements in a virtual public place in regard to students' efforts. When learners see the facilitator investing in this effort, they are more likely to follow suit in their conversations with one another.

- **Cultures of trust:** Trust is never developed overnight. It represents an ongoing effort. Without a sense of trust, learners will not take risks to expand their learning. Therefore, you have to create a learning environment in which learners feel safe to ask questions and interact with their instructor and each other. In other words, you have to focus on building a network of support for learning within the online classroom (Rogo & Portillo, 2015). You can do this by teaching learners how to listen and respond to one another using a perspective-taking approach that entertains and embraces a myriad of possible perspectives, while providing feedback in a manner that is content and not person centered. Providing direct guidance and modeling strategies for communication in a mature and thoughtful manner go a long way in building a classroom in which learners feel safe and open to expand their learning opportunities.

- **Capacity:** Facilitators should consistently monitor the degree to which student capacities are being expanded, either individually or in relationship to team outcomes (Li & Choi, 2014). Most pedagogical experts agree that one best practice for instructors to follow in face-to-face, synchronous learning environments is to tailor questions for students in relationship to their skill, confidence, and overall readiness to participate—their capacity. For example, you might call on students who are not particularly confident to respond to questions that either don't demand background knowledge they may be lacking or are at a level that the students *can* answer. Conversely, if students are ready, tailor particularly challenging questions for them to test their outer limits.

In a cyber-asynchronous-discussion thread, if you see a post from a less confident student, complement him or her, and request elaboration on an already correct point. If you see a more advanced student answer the question rather lazily, challenge him or her with the presentation of a unique inquiry or request. This gives you a chance to make the conversation and the learning come alive.

It is imperative that we invest in the community in order to enhance learning capacity, growth, and engagement (Rogo & Portillo, 2015). Investing in the community, and constantly assessing learning capacity, requires a focus on tailoring instruction to meet learner needs; offering resources to help learners connect meaningfully to the content; and offering timely, relevant, and constructive feedback to support, redirect, and enrich the lesson content (Wei & Chen, 2012). Constantly striving for improved capacity keeps the stakes high, and necessary rigor is more likely to emerge.

Keeping these four Cs in mind helps sustain momentum and promote enhanced connections and communication.

Conclusion

Human beings are meant to connect and collaborate, and we tend to be more successful working in a tribe than working alone. Online communication comes with its own set of rules and pitfalls, so understanding how to help your students facilitate collaborative efforts with you and with each other is paramount in ensuring your online class functions and serves their needs. This is why we encourage you to invest in maintaining course momentum with strategic attention to teaming, collaboration, and enhancements to connect with the students you serve. Sometimes, despite your best efforts, online communication turns toxic. We talk about how you can manage and overcome this particular challenge in the next chapter.

CHAPTER 7

Managing and Overcoming Toxic Conversations

As you have learned in this book, many factors drive momentum in a virtual learning environment, including well-facilitated threaded conversations. In chapter 6, we talked about some steps you can take as a facilitator to ensure that the conversations you have in the course are thoughtful and productive. However, one of the most pressing challenges that instructors face is when these conversations turn negative or toxic. If you've spent any time online looking at public comments on web articles or participating in social media, you've seen how ugly online discourse can get. Without proper facilitation from you, this can happen equally quickly in an online classroom. Therefore, this chapter's purpose is to arm you with perspectives and approaches to deal with toxic conversations in your virtual learning environment and prevent them from spiraling out of control.

KEY QUESTIONS ANSWERED IN THIS CHAPTER

- How can you prevent negative or toxic conversations?
- What are the signs of a negative or toxic conversation in an online classroom?
- What strategic steps can you take to reduce or eliminate negative or toxic interactions in an online classroom?
- What strategic steps do you take if distractions are particularly egregious?

Your goal as a facilitator is to encourage as many positive, productive, and engaging conversations as possible. In order to reach this goal, it is helpful to understand how conversations can move away from this exalted expectation.

Bad Conversations

It's not always a clear-cut line between a productive, if contentious discussion, and one that is about to turn toxic. Learning to differentiate the former from the latter is a key skill for any facilitator in an online classroom. Consider these seven conversation archetypes that describe how online classroom conversations can go wrong.

1. **Lack of formality:** There is a constructive, thoughtful tenor to discussion in a healthy online classroom, one that is focused on learning and new discoveries. This pursuit can be done with a smile. However, texting and other interactions in social media sometimes communicate the message that working in a digital environment makes it OK to use language driven by slang, communicate in incomplete sentences, and perhaps utilize an inordinate amount of abbreviations or shortcuts that are more appropriate for texting than a learning environment. We encourage facilitators to maintain a friendly, formal, and yet approachable tone. You should likewise write in complete sentences and require that students do the same.

2. **High levels of distraction:** In threaded conversations related to particular elements of your learning environment, it is essential that the students remain on task. Students should feel free to ask questions and move away at times from the centrality of focus associated with the learning objectives, but you may find that certain students consistently move away from the main focus of the course and choose to discuss unrelated topics. These distractions are particularly problematic in asynchronous threaded discussions as students attempt to read the threads and catch up with the conversation. A distracting comment can actually have a cascading effect in that multiple readers will likely read and reflect on the distraction, making them less likely to communicate again in a more focused manner. Left unchecked, this can lead to complete derailment of the actual topic discussion and conflict between students who do want to focus on the topic and those focused on the distraction.

3. **Sarcastic commentary:** Whether for the sake of humor or simply in response to a comment learners disagree with, sarcasm in an online learning environment diminishes the learning experience's integrity and can cause conflict among participants. Oftentimes, the way a message is phrased creates the impression of sarcasm where none is intended. In

whatever way sarcasm manifests itself, it distracts learners and can easily make them feel personally attacked. When that happens, the target of the sarcasm often responds in kind, resulting in discourse that quickly spirals into toxicity.

4. **Flirtatious or slightly racy commentary:** If, in a threaded commentary, a student reflects on an exchange with flirty or subtly suggestive commentary, this can result in a rather significant distraction. How to respond as a facilitator depends on the severity of the reactions to the comments and the degree to which they distract from student learning.

5. **Confrontational conversations:** Some learners choose to post confrontational messages on a consistent basis. These messages create a threatening and derisive environment.

6. **Mocking conversations:** Mocking conversations are different than sarcasm. Sarcasm may be conveyed subtly as a form of simply trying to lighten the mood. Although it is destructive, it is not as potentially derailing to the learning experience as mocking behaviors. Mocking behaviors include comments in which an individual (or several individuals) is diminished or demeaned or his or her perspective is diminished or made fun of. This is textbook bullying, as we'll discuss later in this chapter, and it represents a threat that is highly disruptive to quality learning.

7. **Vulgarities (or double entendres):** Many vulgarities (or use of inappropriate double entendres) at the K–12 level revolve around some form of flirtatiousness or sexual innuendo. Other types of vulgarities may likewise diminish or minimize the effectiveness of the learning environment. This is yet another example of a bad conversation pattern that can reduce the effectiveness of in-course dialogue.

The unfortunate reality is that even in the professional world, adults have trouble avoiding interjecting toxic behaviors into online discourse. Your K–12 classroom is filled with students who are only just learning the power of their words to affect those around them. As a facilitator, it's not just your job to establish healthy discourse from the outset but also to ensure that you immediately address behaviors that lead to toxicity in a manner that restores healthy, productive communication among all students. To do that, you have to understand where these behaviors begin and why they occur.

The Roots of Challenging Behaviors

In this section, we reflect on four causes of toxic and negative conversation patterns. Understanding these problems' roots is a first step in reflecting on strategies for dealing with these issues.

1. **Familiarity:** Depending on the circumstance in which you are working, it is possible that the students you are working with know each other from previous interactions and have already established at least some method for regular and ongoing communication. Never forget that you're in their world, not vice versa. In blended classrooms, they probably already know each other on a face-to-face basis, but even students in a distance learning environment may already be connected on Twitter, Facebook, Instagram, or some other social platform. For them, the presentation of your classroom is simply another opportunity to connect. This is problematic because they may already have preexisting patterns of communication they prefer to continue (even inadvertently) in your virtual learning space. There may be preexisting toxicity in their interactions that carries forward into your classroom. Furthermore, the students you serve likely grew up digital, and as a result, they may be more familiar with online communication than you are.

2. **Off-hours interaction:** One of the important elements we need to remember regarding working in an online learning environment is the fact that learners work in the classroom during hours that may not be consistent with the traditional work or school week. Some learners may find themselves working very early, before school hours, while others may work very late. Furthermore, in addition to these different time frames, learners may physically find themselves in very different environments. Learning theorists recognize that the learning context in which we find ourselves can have an impact on our learning (Choi, van Merriënboer, & Paas, 2014). For example, you may have heard before that studying in the lecture hall in which the test will be given puts students in a better position to recall the information when they take the test. There is learning theory to suggest that the location or physical surroundings in which you embed the learning into your brain ultimately stimulates retrieval of that information as it is required (Choi et al., 2014).

    In this context, students may be working in their homes or places where they find themselves unusually relaxed or comfortable. In some instances, this results in better work, but it can also result in some particularly inappropriate impulses toward negative correspondence. For example, it is not uncommon today for a K–12 student to be logged into a computer doing homework, while at the same time logged into several social networking applications. They may have constant pop-ups from multiple instant messaging platforms. A friend may be asking a student what he or she wants to do over the weekend. Students may engage in some sort of gaming activity or stream a movie on a second screen while also working in your classroom on your homework assignment. Despite what kids and teenagers may tell you, the ability to multitask is actually very limited in the human brain (Perkins, 2015; Wieth & Burns, 2014). As a result, the more casual context students experience in other online environments often carries over into their work in your classroom. This is yet another vector that can lead to inappropriate conversations occurring at night or off-school hours, when students may be carrying their social communication directly over into your classroom due to both their familiarity with each other and the context in which they are working at the moment.

3. **Boredom:** As we have alluded to many times in stressing the importance of maintaining interest and enthusiasm, boredom can be significantly problematic in an online learning space. To that end, if a particular discussion thread or request for communication lacks the sufficient capacity to challenge learners, there is much greater opportunity for conversations to go astray and for inappropriate commentary to emerge. Just as you may have experienced in facilitating live classroom discussions in a face-to-face context, in many cases off-task behavior becomes more likely if you make mistakes in the classroom or fail to prepare. Although everyone makes mistakes, your mission should be to avoid them and, even more important, avoid repeating them. If you notice students misbehaving in your virtual learning space, your preparation and enhanced approach to providing an engaging lesson can and should make a significant difference.

4. **Inability to learn:** Students misbehave in a variety of environments if they do not feel they have the capacity to learn or do not believe that they can perform as required. We talked about growth and fixed mindsets in chapter 5, and these sorts of fixed mindsets can be particularly debilitating to students who lack confidence. This lack of confidence often turns into an implicit desire to distract and, in some cases, degrade the learning environment. Bizarrely, to these students, this becomes a more rewarding proposition than to continue to navigate the classroom with (in their minds) very little opportunity to be successful (Dweck, 2015).

At this point, you understand how to recognize bad or toxic communication in your classroom. You understand some of the reasons students inevitably end up engaging in toxic behaviors. Although we do talk later in this chapter about fixing these behaviors and returning your classroom discourse to healthy, productive ground, let's first talk about preventing these behaviors in the first place.

Plan to Prevent Toxic Behaviors

Any doctor will tell you that an ounce of prevention is worth a pound of cure. The same is true in facilitating healthy discourse in your online classroom. Part of that facilitation requires preventing toxic discourse from taking root in the first place. Here is a list of five strategies that are particularly effective in minimizing the opportunity for off-task behaviors.

1. **Institute (and announce) an e-course safe harbor:** Students must understand the rules of the game. Announcing in very certain terms that your e-classroom is a safe harbor, void of bullying, sarcasm, vulgarity, harassment, and all matters of inappropriate communication, represents a direct statement that all virtual instructors should make (see figure 7.1). Announcing this notion of a safe harbor in your introduction to the class and making it part of your syllabus are two very proactive steps. Again, we recommend that you take time in the class to actually connect with students and speak with them about the appropriate interactions you expect. It is a lot better to announce a safe harbor and to clarify expectations up front than to try to respond after inappropriate behaviors have already emerged.

Greetings Class,

As we get started on this learning journey, I would like to take a moment to share a couple of important rules with you regarding how we communicate with one another in this course. In order to have a positive and productive learning experience, it is imperative that each one of you put on your work hat and correspond in a professional manner at all times. This means that words you may use informally (such as at home or with your friends) are not permitted in the classroom. All messages and correspondence within the course room must be honest and open (meaning a school person can understand it), respectful, straightforward, and academic in nature. If you ever have a question about something that you want to say and are not sure if you should post it or say it in class, feel free to message me, and I can discuss this with you.

Ms. Smith

Figure 7.1: Safe harbor announcement.

2. **Demand transparency:** Although students are certainly permitted to be themselves, you must make clear that they are not permitted under any circumstances to communicate with one another—via email, classroom discussion area, or in any other DEL modality—utilizing coded language or jargon that may be unclear to the instructor. As a facilitator, you should make it clear that if you are unable to understand the message or abbreviations, then the student is communicating inappropriately. You need to explain that it is their job to make sure that all correspondence you observe is clear and understandable. If you see such inappropriate communication, reach out to the student or students engaged in that behavior (see figure 7.2).

Hi Mike,

I noticed that you made a couple of comments in the classroom that I was unable to decipher. The comments contained abbreviations that appear to be code words that were meant for a couple of students in the course. I am not sure what those words mean, but I would like to take this opportunity to remind you that all messages in this course must be honest and open (straightforward) and directly relevant to what we are working on in the class. If you plan to communicate with your friends in an informal way, please do so using other communication modalities and not the classroom. Also, because of the nature of those messages, and for the safety and security of the students in the class, I am taking them down and asking that you repost the messages that do not contain code words. I am available to talk if you would like to discuss this matter further. Simply instant message me with a time you would like to meet. Thank you.

Mr. Jones

Figure 7.2: Example of redirecting a student to appropriate classroom communication.

3. **Expect adherence to school rules:** Whether it's a distance learning or blended classroom, remind students that, regardless of their location, when working in the online space as students in your classroom, they are very much operating under the auspices of the school's student code of conduct (or whatever name your school has adopted for the school rules). Assuming board approval, or whatever applies, remind them of the seriousness of that document and that their behaviors in this virtual learning space will be treated as they would if they occurred in a face-to-face learning space.

To highlight the importance of reminding students that all correspondence in the online classroom is school business, consider the following example. Several years ago, while working as a central office administrator, Casey was made aware of a personal student-to-student email exchange in which one of the students indicated his plan to kill a principal. In applying the code of conduct to that scenario, the student's actions ostensibly took place on school grounds, in that the exchange occurred on school property (the district server). Suffice it to say, the police were called in on the exchange, and because the student made the threat via school property, the code of conduct was applied rigorously in this situation, and the student received appropriate school punishment, in addition to criminal charges. Clearly, the student did not think an email exchange would be considered on school grounds. This is why delivering information regarding conduct is critical.

4. **Advise that all content is saved:** One of the more interesting elements of distance learning endeavors is the durability of the actions we take. If we make a mistake as an instructor in a face-to-face lecture, the words may come and go and the mistaken date or misplaced fact may be quickly forgotten or explained away as a verbal misstep. However, when we publish a mistake, unfortunately it lives in perpetuity online. The same is true for any inappropriate comments in the online learning environment. Even when you can retroactively edit messages you post, your original mistake can live on should someone do something as simple as capture it in a screenshot. Students must be told that whatever they say in a digital learning space will be there forever and available for retrieval at any point by members of the district technology department.

5. **Put technology guidelines in place:** Most students are required to sign technology guidelines to ensure that they are aware of the appropriate (and inappropriate) behaviors related to technology. Reminding them of these technology expectations to prevent inappropriate commentary is helpful. One of the most serious issues that students must keep in mind is that their behaviors are not only subject to the student code of conduct, but certain violations can result in significant legal challenges. As we already highlighted, making physical threats can be actionable, depending on their intensity. If students were to upload illegally downloaded files or inappropriate pictures (including nudity or criminal behavior, such as underage drinking), this can result in serious legal repercussions. Most students have come across this type of information or behavior online with other students, if they haven't also played a part in it. What makes this type of infraction most unnerving is the fact that

teachers can openly be held to an even greater degree of responsibility because of the presence of a written word. Judges and juries tend to acknowledge that a recollection of a conversation isn't as powerful as written evidence. Screenshots and other data captures can bring an otherwise ignored or missed malfeasance to light. Being unaware of those activities probably won't appear to be much of an excuse.

There are behaviors in face-to-face communication that, while unproductive, are easy for students and facilitators alike to get away with. It's easy, as a facilitator, to avoid conflict and let inappropriate discourse in your online classroom slide by. This almost never turns out well in the long term, so let this portion of the book be yet another reminder of the importance you must place on reinforcing the seriousness of appropriate online classroom behavior to students as they integrate even more with district systems and technology in the e-learning environment.

Academic Cyberbullying in Threaded Conversations

If you are a teacher in K–12 education, you have undoubtedly heard of cyberbullying. You have, without question, served students in your class who have been the victim of, or participated in, cyberbullying. In many cases, this behavior exists outside your control (Reason, Boyd, & Reason, 2016). That said, you should review your school or district policy regarding cyberbullying, if it has one, for ways you can support victims and help prevent bullying in the first place. As a facilitator in online learning environments, it is important that you recognize the fact that forms of this bullying behavior can actually emerge in threaded conversations inside your classroom.

Be sure to carefully monitor threaded conversations to prevent this from happening. Although it is not always easy, try to peruse all of the threads as they emerge. In particular, look for scenarios where there are multiple respondents to one student's commentary. While this may be the sign of an energetic discussion, which you should encourage, it may also be a sign of bullying. A student in your class may have been bullied in another social networking setting, and that virtual bullying behavior may cross over to a threaded discussion if you are not aware of it and prepared to intervene.

Plan to Respond to Inappropriate Posts and Toxic or Negative Conversations

To this point, we have discussed steps you can take to prevent negative behaviors from occurring. These steps will reduce the volume of negative discourse in your classroom, but they cannot entirely prevent it. As educators, we know that no matter how hard we try, students will make mistakes. Given enough time, we know that negative and toxic conversations will emerge. So, let's talk about a simple three-level process you can use in response to inappropriate threaded conversations. Although productive responses to negative human behavior can be as varied as the reasons people engage in such behavior, we suspect that one of these three levels will work in the vast majority of situations in which you find yourself dealing with harmful, or at least distracting, behaviors.

Reteach and Redirect

Reserve level-one intervention for relatively minor behavior that shows only the potential for causing a distraction. For example, if you notice a less-than-scholarly student tone or a conversation thread veering off course, provide a friendly intervention and perhaps a reintroduction of an element of content in order to bring the conversation back to where it belongs. Whenever possible, take this action with a friendly, professional, and positive tone. Remember, even though this entire chapter is devoted to responding to negative situations, be sure that your attempt to preserve the learning environment does not come off so heavy-handed that students no longer want to communicate openly. In particular, understand the age and mindsets of your students and engage with them on a level that generates productive, healthy responses from them. This is a careful balancing act.

Direct Intervention

At this level, you may observe some behaviors that you believe require direct intervention. In other words, for a level-one response, you may notice that the students are off task, and rather than discussing the behavior, you simply redirect students toward the learning. The level-two response, however, is reserved for behaviors that you believe are serious enough to warrant a discussion of the offense before the redirection back to learning and content. For example, consider the conversation thread in figure 7.3.

> **Tim:** I never understood what they meant on the news by the Electoral College. Now that I learned about it, it makes sense to me, and I can see where it makes statewide voting more equitable in states that don't have as many people.
>
> **Tina:** Yes, but I think the Electoral College system just sucks! You'd have to be an idiot not to be in favor of just counting the votes and picking the winner! It's common sense!

Instructor: Tina, you are welcome to share an alternative perspective regarding the Electoral College system. However, please make sure to use a professional tone and appropriate language. Words like "sucks" and "idiot," even if not directed at anyone in particular, are insulting to people who may have those perspectives—and I do not want that. Try rephrasing your commentary in a more scholarly tone, using more professional and academic language as to why you think the Electoral College is a poor system.

Figure 7.3: Example of a level-two direct intervention.

Notice how the instructor intervened and spoke specifically to the inappropriate behavior, making it clear exactly what the student did wrong, and publicly redirected the conversation in a more positive way. The advantage of this public exchange is that it gives the instructor a chance to reinforce for the entire class his or her expectations. In this case, the teacher did not view the use of the word *sucks* as being particularly egregious. It was not the tone she wanted, but she did not feel the need to delete the thread or punish the student. It was simply a teachable moment; she thought the student simply needed a bit of support to return to the right track.

Direct and Serious Intervention

There are, of course, instances in which the infraction is much more egregious than a simple thread derailment or failure to communicate effectively. If a student uses profanity, makes a threat, or follows up with any of the negative conversation examples provided earlier in a way that simply cannot be allowed in the classroom, the level-three response is the next logical step. In this case, it is imperative that you eliminate the comment. For example, if a student made a vulgar or sexual comment about a female student in the class, it would be incredibly inappropriate to allow that comment to remain a part of the classroom. In that context, the sooner you can remove the comment, the better. If the commentary was particularly egregious, it may be necessary to eliminate the entire thread. If one student made one comment that is slightly out of line, and you want to take it out, simply removing that artery within the conversation can be effective.

Depending on the vulgarity of the statement, you may need to immediately apply the student code of conduct. Examine this decision pursuant to the climate of discipline in the school. For the sake of learning and the construction of a positive virtual learning culture, removing damaging, destructive, or inappropriate comments is non-negotiable. If we as instructors fail to remove these comments, we are tacitly participating in the humiliation of the students involved, not to mention the fact that we open the door for that toxicity to escalate. We cannot emphasize enough the critical importance of not only modeling appropriate online behavior for your students, but ensuring that every student in your class engages his or her classmates in an appropriate way.

Conclusion

Preserving the sanctity of communication in your online classroom is critical to ensuring student success. Whether your students are young children or teenagers burgeoning on adulthood, they're all at some stage of learning how to communicate with you and their peers. You can help them along that path by employing the strategies in this chapter to prevent the incursion of toxic discourse. When you have students stray from that path, as they inevitably will, it's important to recognize early the types of communication that lead to increased toxicity and then implement an appropriate response. There is no perfect formula for choosing your level of response, so trust your instinct and use the strategies in this chapter. Think about how you might react in the face-to-face classroom. It is important for those of us who did not grow up learning online to remember that just because it occurs online, the activity is no less serious than if it were happening in your face-to-face classroom, right in front of you. Taking this seriously and attempting to prevent and respond to these behaviors will result in a much better classroom for everyone involved.

CHAPTER 8

Concluding the Learning Experience

The steps we take to conclude our learning experience make a difference in terms of just how much learners retain and what they do with their new knowledge and skills once the course is over. This is true in just about any learning venue you can imagine. The purpose of this chapter, therefore, is to reflect on some best-practice approaches you can take to help maximize the learning experience as it comes to fruition.

KEY QUESTIONS ANSWERED IN THIS CHAPTER

- What steps can you take to conclude the learning experience?
- How do your concluding actions impact future learning?

It's unfortunately common for facilitators in online environments to neglect to provide closure for learners by ending the course with a declaration of the final assignment deadline. The students in these scenarios log off when they are done and never look back. We believe this reinforces a sense of isolation and disconnect for learners. Even in cases where students have met all their objectives, the lack of a specific and discernable finality takes away from the level of connection the facilitator established throughout the course. Not surprisingly, facilitators who do very little to conclude their courses are oftentimes relatively poor at creating a culture or climate in the course itself that is conducive to positive interactions and learning. Let's look at some ways you can avoid this pitfall in facilitating the end of your own online class.

The Power of Writing and Learning Consolidation

As we have said earlier in this book, writing is a very powerful tool in helping to organize your thoughts. As an educator, you already understand that you only really begin to know and understand a topic once you have to create written documents either describing it or articulating your thoughts regarding the content area. This is a neurological process we call *consolidation*.

It's easy to forget that at any given moment our brains are exposed to an incalculable amount of stimuli going on around us. Even while you read the words in this book, there are sounds going on around you and other experiences (recent or otherwise) on your mind that are competing for your attention. In learning, the consolidation process involves taking all of these competing stimuli and deciding what to keep, store, revisit, and reinforce—and what to let go (Harris, 2014; Steiner, 2009). Anyone who has crammed for a test can recall that empty feeling when you recognize that indeed you were able to repeat the information quickly during the assessment but were unable to apply that information later. You had too much intel coming in at once, and because there wasn't meaning associated with the cramming, your brain simply didn't see the value in the information and dumped it out.

In the case of an online learning experience, we can't guarantee that learners will hang on to the learning you provide with a greater degree of fidelity than you would find in a physical classroom. Certainly, there are face-to-face experiences that can bring a great sense of emotion to the learning that allows some of those experiences to truly last a lifetime. However, as we have consistently pointed out in this book, there are a number of meaningful learning experiences you can have online that can make a significant impact. Furthermore, what we have learned about the consolidation process is that it is significantly impacted by writing and reflecting, two factors you can emphasize in an online curriculum (Beveridge, Fruchter, Sanmartin, & deLottinville, 2014; Embo, Driessen, Valcke, & Van Der Vleuten, 2014).

Asking learners to write about their experiences certainly is a well-heeled strategy that has had success. In this context, we recommend that you ask learners to directly and purposefully reflect on their learning experiences. In particular, we believe that many of the experiences you facilitate to conclude the online learning course can and should revolve around opportunities for the learners to reflect on their learning in an attempt to stimulate this consolidating piece of the learning process.

Student Reflection

Reflection, too, is a key part of the consolidation process. We recommend that you take the opportunity at the end of the course to review the major learning objectives.

The level of the learners you serve should determine the depth of this review. As a baseline, revisiting the major goals and asking the learners to evaluate the degree to which they achieved proficiency in these important areas will pay significant dividends in terms of consolidating the learning.

As part of this review, remind those in your course that learning is not an all-or-nothing proposition. If learners have the chance at the end of your curriculum to reflect on a variety of topics and evaluate which learning outcomes they feel they most thoughtfully mastered and which they are still working on, then you are helping them think critically about their learning and themselves; hopefully, this reflection continues after the moment they log out.

For example, you may have offered a wonderfully interactive simulation early in the course that the learners enjoyed and remembered and through which they learned new skills or sensibilities. Asking them to reflect on that experience later in the course, in relationship to what you are currently covering, may actually reinforce the learning once again and perhaps solidify that learning experience to a greater and ultimately more durable level (from a learning perspective). Examples of questions you might pose to students at the end of the course to nurture learning consolidation and to help them extend their learning include the following.

- What have you learned in this course that you can use in your own life?

- In what ways will you use what you learned in the course?

- What additional topics in the area of _____ would you like to explore?

- What was the most interesting thing you learned during this class, and why was it so interesting to you?

- What topic that we explored in this class do you believe you could teach to others, and how would you teach it to them?

Questions like these work because the very act of asking students to reflect on their learning stimulates the consolidation process and activates their learning systems to reinforce certain elements or experiences.

Facilitator Reflection

As you have learned throughout this book, the online learning environment provides facilitators with unique formative elements called breadcrumbs (learning evidence) of student work based on virtually every interaction that the student leaves behind in the virtual classroom. Given this, as you manage the concluding activities for your course, take some time to reflect on your own performance. For example, in reading a class's reflections on a particular element of the learning experience, the facilitator may be able to carefully examine students' word choices to determine with greater degrees of certainty just how impactful his or her instructional approaches may be.

Consider the following example of how student reflection might be used to enhance the learning experience. In a post on the discussion board designated for reflection on a particular book the class read, Amy says, "I really enjoyed reading this book. I was a little confused when the author had the main character turn his adopted brother into the authorities because in a previous chapter the main character said he couldn't stand the police. It was confusing to me that the author would have the main character do something that seemed completely different than what you would expect him to do. I never do things that are against my principles, so I don't understand why he would change his mind."

Johnny replies, "I hated this book. It was boring. I also did not like that Will turned his adopted brother into the police when he said many times throughout the book that he didn't like the police. It didn't make any sense. I also didn't like that Will dumped his girlfriend for no reason. That didn't make any sense either. There was no explanation for it that I could see."

In reading over the student reflections, the teacher can determine that both students were able to sufficiently analyze text and were able to provide evidence that their understanding of the text was extended well beyond basic comprehension. Both learners were confused by the turn of events that happened at the end. From here the facilitator could extend the conversation with the learners and ask them if they could rewrite the ending, how would they do so, and why? The facilitator could also use this as a teaching moment for writing conclusions within a story or essay, the importance of good organization, and staying true to theme when authoring text.

Suffice it to say, this opportunity gives facilitators a unique perspective on their own performance and allows them to go back, analyze answers, and truly think much more comprehensively about their work than in a face-to-face environment. What is also unique to this type of experience is the ability to go back and ask the students for clarification and to engage in dialogue with them at a deeper level regarding a certain element of the course in which the students share their experiences or reflections.

Activities to Strengthen Course Conclusion

Once again, we believe that just about any type of thoughtful conclusion educators bring to their traditional face-to-face courses can be executed in an online learning environment. Not only that, but we think there are examples of concluding activities that are *more* effective in this modality. Let's take a look at three of them.

1. **Portfolio presentation, management, and transition:** Because online learning often provides a far more organized and efficient mechanism for establishing and maintaining a portfolio, learners are able to more easily look at their past assignments and reflect on their growth. In this context, having these digital tools available makes it easier to ask learners to reflect on the work they have done and to specifically reference their key areas of growth.

    Portfolios also allow the facilitator to more effectively negotiate the transition as the learner moves from one class to another. For example, if a learner from the middle school level is moving from a sixth-grade learning experience in language arts to seventh grade, this modality helps ease and magnify that transition because the inherited instructor suddenly has tools available for observing the work that came before. This allows the new instructor to quickly get up to speed in terms of the types of supports the learner may need to continue to grow and improve.

2. **Source sharing and learning extensions:** As the course comes to a conclusion, take the opportunity to show learners how they can continue to extend their learning and, if that learning ignited areas of interest for them, to continue to pursue growth in that area. For example, a science learner might have been particularly engaged during team activities in an astronomy lesson. As a point of conclusion and transition to the next level, a facilitator might remind her or him of that experience and provide some additional sources of learning about astronomy, thus encouraging the student to continue to learn more about it. Although there are certainly some learners who will pass over an opportunity like this, we cannot ignore the possibility that this small amount of encouragement might take a spark of interest and transition it into a flame-driven, passionate pursuit that ultimately shapes the learner's career and life trajectory. Certainly, by sharing sources and inviting opportunities to grow, we further consolidate the learning as well.

3. **Network building:** Even if learners are relatively familiar with their classmates, we recommend that you encourage them at the end of the course, even at younger ages, to solidify connections with their classmates and to continue to build that network. As a facilitator, you devote a lot of your time and energy to building constructive discourse in your online classroom. This is yet another way those efforts can pay off for your students. In a contemporary, highly networked professional learning environment, where colleagues meet each other at a distance, without boundaries of time and space, students need to be adept at

making and nurturing connections that will help them innovate, create systems for networking, and build their capacity for personal and professional communication and growth. Figure 8.1 offers an example.

Review

Why is it that LinkedIn is so popular? It has taken professional networking to a new level. Not only can you connect with professionals with whom you have relationships, but you can connect with their connections and virtually shake hands with professionals all over the world. Think for a moment how this benefits people and organizations. Networking is the backbone of success, both personally and professionally.

Take a moment to discuss with your team members where they would like to go in their personal and professional lives and consider how your personal and professional goals may intersect with theirs. Consider how many connections you can make with others to help them reach their goals. When you have completed this activity, submit a statement, as a group, about how you can help each other in the future and how a connection within a network could benefit all in your group.

Figure 8.1: Network-building activity.

End With a Smile

We strongly encourage you to end your course with a public acknowledgment at its conclusion that expresses appreciation for the learning opportunities the participants shared. You could even launch this public bon voyage via video to help bring a greater degree of personalization to that experience. A written message, like the example in figure 8.2, also works.

Greetings Class,

As we conclude the year, I can't help but reflect how great it has been to work with each one of you! In exploring different elements of the U.S. government, and some of the foundational moments of the history of the United States, I hope that you have had the opportunity to better understand your country!

Throughout this class, I was really impressed with how thoughtful you were during our discussion and debates. Your tone was always professional, mature, and thoughtful. Furthermore, you all learned to use primary sources! As you move forward I encourage you to use what you learned about debating in other classes and in your own personal life. I hope that you can be just as thoughtful when talking to your friends or family members as you have demonstrated in here! As you can see, you learned a lot more by listening and collaborating!

It's been an honor to work with you and I wish you the best of luck.

Ms. Smith

Figure 8.2: Sample conclusion.

As you can see Ms. Smith ended with a smile. She reminded the students of how far they have come and encouraged them to give thought to how they could apply their learning. Students that read this type of message repeatedly will reflect on how much they have grown and the work they put in to get there. It's also easy to see, from reading this message, how much Ms. Smith cares about her students!

Conclusion

The manner in which you end a course makes a big difference in how students move forward. We encourage you to take copious notes throughout your own experience and to continue to fine-tune your performance as you go. For example, you may recall that certain activities have resulted in an unexpectedly low or high level of student engagement. Obviously, this is something you can monitor and use to make adjustments. You may also have discovered that a specific learning intervention or source might have been helpful to your students. Collecting these notes along the way has always been a good idea in any teaching environment, but it's arguably even more essential in a digital learning space. The ability to evaluate your learning impact on students in your time together can obviously make a big difference in your own growth as a facilitator of learning online.

Concluding Thoughts

Like most of you reading this book, we can recall formative learning experiences in our lives that changed our paradigms forever. When Casey was in graduate school, his professor, Leigh Chiarelott (2016), gave a lecture that we've adapted here.

WHY CAN'T SCHOOLS BE MORE LIKE AMUSEMENT PARKS?

In Phillip W. Jackson's (1968) book *Life in Classrooms*, he coined the term hidden curriculum and compared schools metaphorically to prisons and mental hospitals. He noted that schools resemble these institutions because one group (prisoners, patients, students) are involuntarily committed to these institutions while another, more privileged group (guards, interns, teachers) have the right to leave any time, and are placed in the position of "guarding the exits, both literally and figuratively." While this comparison may seem unduly harsh to some, it does merit some consideration in light of how many children view their thirteen-year "sentence" to schooling.

Amusement parks, on the other hand, are designed primarily to be fun for both children and adults and offer a wide variety of entertainment options to meet the needs of all who venture in. Adults accompany children and guide them, often encouraging them to try out a new ride or attraction and to take risks without fear of punishment or failure. If the child doesn't enjoy the ride or attraction, he or she simply does not choose to repeat the experience. Like many experiences that initially don't elicit a positive response, the rides and attractions may become more enjoyable at a later age or

CONTINUED →

stage of development and the child and adult can always revisit that experience at a later date. Ultimately, with adult guidance, the child can choose the experience he or she needs or wants and either come back to it repeatedly or simply move on to something else. The intent of the amusement park is for everyone to enjoy the experience, try something new or repeat a prior positive experience, and to leave the park tired but happy. I would suggest that any school that has that intent, and results in all who enter it as leaving tired but happy at the end of the day, would not only be a highly successful school but a high-performing school. Has the time come to embrace a new metaphor for schools?

We like this illustration because we believe that our beliefs and paradigms are the first things we must change in order to enhance learning—digitally or otherwise. We hope your approach to teaching and learning draws on aspirations of making learning fun, challenging, and engaging, for you and for your students. Thankfully, digital tools make the evolution of this more dynamic, engaging environment a more likely possibility. It is this ability to evolve that really separates DEL from learning initiatives of the past. Consider the rise and fall of correspondence schools.

Unevolved Learning

Interestingly, several of the most prominent for-profit companies who make their living in adult digital learning started off as correspondence schools. Throughout much of 20th century, correspondence schools were quite a popular choice in terms of learning a new skill or developing a new personal or professional competency. The correspondence school experience consisted of the following four steps.

1. The school sends books and supplemental materials and assessments to the client.

2. The client reads the book, perhaps watches a VHS tape, takes a test and writes a paper, and then sends the test and paper back to the correspondence school.

3. The correspondence school unpacks the student's assessment and sends it to a grader. That grader takes the time to assess the material and sends it back to the correspondence school with the results.

4. The school sends the results back to the student.

When email became an affordable solution, things began to change and correspondence schools simplified all of the aforementioned steps by simply using email instead of the U.S. Postal Service. This change made a big difference in cost effectiveness, organization, and efficiency. However, these tactical changes didn't change the learner's experience or improve the capacity to enhance the deepest learning. It simply made the process more efficient (Harting & Erthal, 2005).

Despite not being focused on K–12 students, this model is relevant to us for two interesting reasons. First, several of these early correspondence schools became early innovators in online learning for adults. Not surprisingly, their modes of operation spawned from the correspondence school experience (Harting & Erthal, 2005). Thus, from an early age, a desire to simply extend the correspondence school modality arguably drove the old online learning model. Although this model might've gotten the ball rolling, as modern educators we need to decisively make sure that we see learning from a far different frame than these origins.

The other lesson we can learn from the correspondence school history is that simply adding technology implements to an old learning model for the sake of efficiency isn't enough. As the next rounds of technology innovation swirl around us, we need to avoid looking at these new tools as clever bells and whistles to be utilized to dress up antiquated approaches. Everything we've shared about DEL in this book must represent a bold willingness to use technology to engage the learning process at higher levels of effectiveness than ever before. This requires us to think differently about how we cultivate our lush gardens of learning.

Brilliant Innovations, Blurred Lines, and Lush Gardens

What lies ahead? How do we avoid repeating the past mistakes of correspondence learning? We actually see a very robust future in terms of our profession's capacity to improve thanks to the emergence of brilliant innovations in DEL. We also predict that as we embrace the concepts of DEL, our culture will be increasingly less in need of even utilizing the term. If futurists are correct, and the 21st century evolves in a way in which technology continues to demonstrate an uncompromisingly robust interconnectivity with our daily lives, we won't have to even use a phrase like *digitally enhanced learning* because it will be assumed that just about everything in our lives, including learning, must be continuously enhanced with the technology around us. For the same reason we stopped using words like *electric typewriter*, there comes a time when the new way of living and working is so fully integrated that it's just assumed.

For now, as we make the transition, it's exceedingly important that we make a clear and distinct departure from the past, put correspondence schools and old visions of learning online at a distance aside, and move toward more thoughtfully constructed environments for online learning. In keeping with the example we presented at the very start of this book, we urge you to reflect on that gardener who utilizes the tools he is given to make his garden flourish like never before. In this case, you are the gardener and this is the time. Strategies for DEL are your tools, and learning is the flourishing garden.

References and Resources

Adriansen, H. K. O., & Madsen, L. M. (2013). Facilitation: A novel way to improve students' well-being. *Innovative Higher Education, 38*(4), 295–308.

Al-Qahtani, A. A., & Higgins, S. (2012). Effects of traditional, blended and e-learning on students' achievement in higher education. *Journal of Computer Assisted Learning, 29*(3), 220–234.

Alvarez, I., Espasa, A., & Guasch, T. (2012). The value of feedback in improving collaborative writing assignments in an online learning environment. *Studies in Higher Education, 37*(4), 387–400.

Amory, A. (2012). Instructivist ideology: Education technology embracing the past? *Interactive Learning Environments, 20*(1), 41–55.

Aparicio, M., Bacao, F., & Oliveira, T. (2016). An e-learning theoretical framework. *Journal of Educational Technology and Society, 19*(1), 292–307.

Artino, A. R. (2009a). Think, feel, act: Motivational and emotional influences on military students' online academic success. *Journal of Computing in Higher Education, 21*, 146–166.

Artino, A. R., Jr. (2009b). Online learning: Are subjective perceptions of instructional context related to academic success? *The Internet and Higher Education, 12*(3–4), 117–125.

Azevedo, R., Moos, D. C., Greene, J. A., Winters, F., & Cromley, J. G. (2008). Why is externally-facilitated regulated learning more effective than self-regulated learning with hypermedia? *Educational Technology Research and Development, 56*(1), 45–72.

Baker, D. J., & Zuvela, D. (2013). Feedforward strategies in the first-year experience of online and distributed learning environments. *Assessment and Evaluation in Higher Education, 38*(6), 687–697.

Basham, J. D., Meyer, H., & Perry, E. (2010). The design and application of the digital backpack. *Journal of Research on Technology in Education, 42*(4), 339–359.

Beveridge, T. S., Fruchter, L. L., Sanmartin, C. V., & deLottinville, C. B. (2014). Evaluating the use of reflective practice in a nonprofessional, undergraduate clinical communication skills course. *Teaching in Higher Education, 19*(1), 58–71.

Brett, P. (2011). Students' experiences and engagement with SMS for learning in higher education. *Innovations in Education and Teaching International, 48*(2), 137–147.

Britt, M., Goon, D., & Timmerman, M. (2015). How to better engage online students with online strategies. *College Student Journal, 49*(3), 399–404.

Brookhart, S. M. (2013). *How to create and use rubrics for formative assessment and grading.* Alexandria, VA: Association for Supervision and Curriculum Development.

Brown, R. E. (2001). The process of community-building in distance learning classes. *Journal of Asynchronous Learning Networks, 5*(2), 18–35.

Bryant, J., & Bates, A. (2015). Creating a constructivist online instructional environment. *TechTrends: Linking Research and Practice to Improve Learning, 59*(2), 17–22.

Bunn, J. (2004). Student persistence in a LIS distance education program. *Australian Academic and Research Libraries, 35*(3), 253–269.

Burnett, B. (2004). Technophiles and technophobes? In B. Burnett, D. Meadmore, & G. Tait (Eds.), *New questions for contemporary teachers: Taking a socio-cultural approach to education.* Frenchs Forest, New South Wales: Pearson Education Australia.

Carter, T., Hardy, C. A., & Hardy, J. C. (2001). Latin vocabulary acquisition: An experiment using information-processing techniques of chunking and imagery. *Journal of Instructional Psychology, 28*(4), 225.

Cavanagh, S. (2014). 'Personalized learning' eludes easy definitions. *Education Week, 34*(9), s2–s4.

The Center for Teaching and Learning, University of North Carolina at Charlotte. (2015). *150 teaching methods.* Accessed at http://teaching.uncc.edu/learning-resources/articles-books/best-practice/instructional-methods/150-teaching-methods on July 7, 2016.

Chen, J., Dai, D. Y., & Zhou, Y. (2013). Enable, enhance, and transform: How technology use can improve gifted education. *Roeper Review, 35*(3), 166–176.

Chen, N.-S., Wei, C.-W., Huany, Y.-C., & Kinshuk. (2013). The integration of print and digital content for providing learners with constructive feedback using smartphones. *British Journal of Educational Technology, 44*(5), 837–845.

Cheng, C. K., Pare, D. E., Collimore, L.-M., & Joordens, S. (2011). Assessing the effectiveness of a voluntary online discussion forum on improving students' course performance. *Computers and Education, 56*(1), 253–261.

Chhabra, R., & Sharma, V. (2013). Applications of blogging in problem based learning. *Education and Information Technologies, 18*(1), 3–13.

Chiarelotte, L. (2016). *Why can't schools be more like amusement parks?* [Lecture]. University of Toledo, Toledo, OH.

Childress, S., & Benson, S. (2014). Personalized learning for every student every day. *Phi Delta Kappan*, *95*(8), 33–38.

Cho, K., & Cho, M.-H. (2013). Training of self-regulated learning skills on a social network system. *Social Psychology of Education*, *16*(4), 617–634.

Cho, M.-H. (2012). Online student orientation in higher education: A developmental study. *Educational Technology Research and Development*, *60*(6), 1051–1069.

Cho, M.-H., & Heron, M. L. (2015). Self-regulated learning: The role of motivation, emotion, and use of learning strategies in students' learning experiences in a self-paced online mathematics course. *Distance Education*, *36*(1), 80–99.

Cho, M.-H., & Shen, D. (2013). Self-regulation in online learning. *Distance Education*, *34*(3), 290–301.

Choi, H.-H., van Merriënboer, J. J. G., & Paas, F. (2014). Effects of the physical environment on cognitive load and learning: Towards a new model of cognitive load. *Educational Psychology Review*, *26*(2), 225–244.

Chu, H. C. (2014). Potential negative effects of mobile learning on students' learning achievement and cognitive load—A format assessment perspective. *Journal of Educational Technology and Society*, *17*(1), 332–344.

Ciampa, K. (2013). Learning in a mobile age: An investigation of student motivation. *Journal of Computer Assisted Learning*, *30*(1), 82–96.

Ciani, K. D., Summers, J. J., Easter, M. A., & Sheldon, K. M. (2008). Collaborative learning and positive experiences: Does letting students choose their own groups matter? *Educational Psychology*, *28*(6), 627–641.

Clark, T., & Barbour, M. K. (2015). Online, blended, and distance education in schools: An introduction. In T. Clark & M. K. Barbour (Eds.), *Online, blended and distance education in schools: Building successful programs* (pp. 3–10). Sterling, VA: Stylus.

Cook, V. (2012). Learning everywhere, all the time. *Delta Kappa Gamma Bulletin*, *78*(3), 48–51.

Cowan, N. (2014). Working memory underpins cognitive development, learning, and education. *Educational Psychology Review*, *26*(2), 197–223.

Crow, M. M. (2013). Digital learning: Look, then leap. *Nature*, *499*(7458), 275–277.

Csikszentmihalyi, M. (1975). *Beyond boredom and anxiety*. San Francisco: Jossey-Bass.

Curry, J. H., & Cook, J. (2014). Facilitating online discussions at a manic pace: A new strategy for an old problem. *Quarterly Review of Distance Education*, *15*(3), 1–12.

Cviko, A., McKenney, S., & Voogt, J. (2012). Teachers enacting a technology-rich curriculum for emergent literacy. *Educational Technology Research and Development*, *60*(1), 31–54.

Davis, M. R. (2015). Online credit recovery in need of overhaul, study says. *Education Week*, *35*(5), 8.

Davis, M. (2016, September 14). Digital citizenship week: 6 resources for educators [Blog post]. Accessed at www.edutopia.org/blog/digital-citizenship-resources-matt-davis on January 3, 2017.

de Jong, T. (2010). Cognitive load theory, educational research and instructional design: Some food for thought. *Instructional Science, 38*, 105–134.

Delialioğlu, Ö. (2011). Student engagement in blended learning environments with lecture-based and problem-based instructional approaches. *Journal of Educational Technology and Society, 15*(3), 310–322.

Desroches, D. (2016, February 29). UConn professor says charter school growth is like subprime mortgage bubble. [Interview]. Accessed at http://wnpr.org/post/uconn-professor-says-charter-school-growth-subprime-mortgage-bubble on March 3, 2016.

Diaz, V. (2010). Web 2.0 and emerging technologies in online learning. *New Directions for Community Colleges,* (150), 57–66.

Driscoll, A., Jicha, K., Hunt, A. N., Tichavsky, L., & Thompson, G. (2012). Can online courses deliver in-class results? *Teaching Sociology, 40*(4), 312–331.

DuFour, R., & Reason, C. (2016). *Professional Learning Communities at Work and virtual collaboration: On the tipping point of transformation.* Bloomington, IN: Solution Tree Press.

Duke, J. M., & Awokuse, T. O. (2009). Assessing the effect of bilateral collaborations on learning outcomes. *Review of Agricultural Economics, 31*(2), 344–358.

Dweck, C. S. (2010). Even geniuses work hard. *Educational Leadership, 68*(1), 16–20.

Dweck, C. S. (2015). The remarkable reach of "growth mind-sets." *Scientific American Mind, 27*(1), 36–41.

Edwards, M., Perry, B., & Janzen, K. (2011). The making of an exemplary online educator. *Distance Education, 32*(1), 101–118.

Ehrmann, S. C. (2013). How technology matters to learning. *Liberal Education, 99*(1), 22–25.

Embo, M. P., Driessen, E., Valcke, M., & Van Der Vleuten, C. P. (2014). Scaffolding reflective learning in clinical practice: A comparison of two types of reflective activities. *Medical Teacher, 36*(7), 602–607.

Eshchar, Y., & Fragaszy, D. (2015). What is teaching? A clear, integrative, operational definition for teaching is still needed. *Behavioral and Brain Sciences, 38*(39), 71.

Evans, D. R., Zeun, P., & Stanier, R. A. (2014). Motivating student learning using a formative assessment journey. *Journal of Anatomy, 224*(3), 296–303.

Evans, P. (2015). Open online spaces of professional learning: Context, personalisation and facilitation. *TechTrends: Linking Research and Practice to Improve Learning, 59*(1), 31–36.

Flett, G. L., & Hewitt, P. L. (2014). A proposed framework for preventing perfectionism and promoting resilience and mental health among vulnerable children and adolescents. *Psychology in the Schools, 51*(9), 899–912.

Fonollosa, J., Neftci, E., & Rabinovich, M. (2015). Learning of chunking sequences in cognition and behavior. *Plos Computational Biology, 11*(11), 1–24.

Friberg, J. C. (2012). Using iPad technologies to support teaching and learning in CSD. *Perspectives on Issues in Higher Education, 15*(1), 16–21.

Gao, F., Zhang, T., & Franklin, T. (2013). Designing asynchronous online discussion environments: Recent progress and possible future directions. *British Journal of Educational Technology, 44*(3), 469–483.

Garrison, D. R., & Arbaugh, J. B. (2007). Researching the community of inquiry framework: Review, issues, and future directions. *The Internet and Higher Education, 10*(3), 157–172.

Garrison, D. R., & Kanuka, H. (2004). Blended learning: Uncovering its transformative potential in higher education. *Internet and Higher Education, 7*(2), 95–105.

Ge, Z.-G. (2012). Cyber asynchronous versus blended cyber approach in distance English learning. *Journal of Educational Technology and Society, 15*(2), 286–297.

Gilmore, S., & Warren, S. (2007). Themed article: Emotion online: Experiences of teaching in a virtual learning environment. *Human Relations, 60*(4), 581–608.

Goodwin, B. (2014). Curiosity is fleeting, but teachable. *Educational Leadership, 72*(1), 73–74.

Gregori, E., Torras, E., & Guasch, T. (2012). Cognitive attainment in online learning environments: Matching cognitive and technological presence. *Interactive Learning Environments, 20*(5), 467–483.

Guest. (2015, May 12). Digital natives demand a retail revolution. *Adweek: Social Times.* Accessed at www.adweek.com/socialtimes/digital-natives-demand-a-retail-revolution/620121 on July 7, 2016.

Hannafin, M., Land, S., & Oliver, K. (1999). Open learning environments: Foundations, methods, and models. In C. M. Reigeluth (Ed.), *Instructional-design theories and models: A new paradigm of theories and models* (Vol. 2, pp. 115–140). Mahwah: NJ: Erlbaum.

Hardré, P. L. (2013). Considering components, types, and degrees of authenticity in designing technology to support transfer. *New Directions for Adult and Continuing Education, 2013*(137), 39–47.

Harrell, I. L., & Bower, B. L. (2011). Student characteristics that predict persistence in community college online courses. *American Journal of Distance Education, 25*(3), 178–191.

Harris, K. D. (2014). Sleep replay meets brain-machine interface. *Nature Neuroscience, 17*(8), 1019–1021.

Harting, K., & Erthal, M. J. (2005). History of distance learning. *Information Technology, Learning, and Performance Journal, 23*(1), 35–44.

Henson, K. T. (2015). *Curriculum planning: Integrating multiculturalism, constructivism, and education reform* (5th ed.). Long Grove, IL: Waveland Press.

Herrington, J., & Parker, J. (2013). Emerging technologies as cognitive tools for authentic learning. *British Journal of Educational Technology, 44*(4), 607–615.

Higgins, S., Mercier, E., Burd, L., & Joyce-Gibbons, A. (2012). Multi-touch tables and collaborative learning. *British Journal of Educational Technology*, *43*(6), 1041–1054.

Hockett, J. A., & Doubet, K. J. (2013). Turning on the lights: What pre-assessments can do. *Educational Leadership*, *71*(4), 50–54.

Hodgson, P., & Pang, M. Y. (2012). Effective formative e-assessment of student learning: A study on a statistics course. *Assessment and Evaluation in Higher Education*, *37*(2), 215–225.

Hoffman, C., & Goodwin, S. (2006). A clicker for your thoughts: Technology for active learning. *New Library World*, *107*(9), 422–433.

Hohmann, J. W., & Grillo, M. C. (2014). Using critical thinking rubrics to increase academic performance. *Journal of College Reading and Learning*, *45*(1), 35–51.

Holzweiss, P. C., Joyner, S. A., Fuller, M. B., Henderson, S., & Young, R. (2014). Online graduate students' perceptions of best learning experiences. *Distance Education*, *35*(3), 311–323.

Horstmanshof, L., & Brownie, S. (2013). A scaffolded approach to discussion board use for formative assessment of academic writing skills. *Assessment and Evaluation in Higher Education*, *38*(1), 61–73.

Hou, H.-T. (2012). Analyzing the learning process of an online role-playing discussion activity. *Journal of Educational Technology and Society*, *15*(1), 211–222.

Howard, L., & Whitaker, M. (2011). Unsuccessful and successful mathematics learning: Developmental students' perceptions. *Journal of Developmental Education*, *35*(2), 2–16.

Hsin, C.-T., Li, M.-C, & Tsai, C.-C. (2014). The influence of young children's use of technology on their learning: A review. *Journal of Educational Technology and Society*, *17*(4), 85–99.

Hsiung, C. M., Luo, L. F., & Chung, H. C. (2014). Early identification of ineffective cooperative learning teams. *Journal of Computer Assisted Learning*, *30*(6), 534–545.

Huang, Y.-M., Liang, T.-H., Su, Y.-N., & Chen, N.-S. (2012) Empowering personalized learning with an interactive e-book learning system or elementary school students. *Educational Technology Research and Development*, *60*(4), 703–722.

Hwang, G.-J., Hung, C.-M., & Chen, N.-S. (2014). Improving learning achievements, motivations and problem-solving skills through a peer assessment-based game development approach. *Educational Technology Research and Development*, *62*(2), 129–145.

Hwang, G.-J., Hung, P.-H, Chen, N.-S, Liu, G.-Z. (2014). Mindtool-assisted in-field learning (MAIL): An advanced ubiquitous learning project in Taiwan. *Journal of Educational Technology and Society*, *17*(2), 4–16.

Hwang, G.-J., Hung, P.-H, Chen, N.-S, Liu, G.-Z. (2014). Mindtool-assisted in-field learning (MAIL): An advanced ubiquitous learning project in Taiwan. *Journal of Educational Technology and Society*, *17*(2), 4–16.

Ioannou, A., & Stylianou-Georgiou, A. (2012). Mashing-up wikis and forums: A case study of collaborative problem-based activity. *Educational Media International, 49*(4), 303–316.

Irwin, B., Hepplestone, S., Holden, G., Parkin, H. J., & Thorpe, L. (2013). Engaging students with feedback through adaptive release. *Innovations in Education and Teaching International, 50*(1), 51–61.

Ivankova, N. V., & Stick, S. L. (2005). Collegiality and community-building as a means for sustaining student persistence in the computer-mediated asynchronous learning environment. *Online Journal of Distance Learning Administration, 8*(3).

Jackson, P. W. (1968). *Life in classrooms.* New York: Holt, Rinehart and Winston.

Jacobson, M. D. (2013). Afraid of looking dumb. *Educational Leadership, 71*(1), 40–43.

Jagger, S. (2013). Affective learning and the classroom debate. *Innovations in Education and Teaching International, 50*(1), 38–50.

Jang, H., Reeve, J., & Deci, E. L. (2010). Engaging students in learning activities: It is not autonomy support or structure but autonomy support and structure. *Journal of Educational Psychology, 102*(3), 588–600.

Järvelä, S., & Hadwin, A. F. (2013). New frontiers: Regulating learning in CSCL. *Educational Psychologist, 48*(1), 25–39.

Jehangir, R. R. (2012). Conflict as a catalyst for learning. *About Campus, 17*(2), 2–8.

Jianzhong, X., Jianxia, D., & Xitao, F. (2015). Students' groupwork management in online collaborative learning environments. *Journal of Educational Technology and Society, 18*(2), 195–205.

Jiao, H. (2015). Enhancing students' engagement in learning through a formative e-assessment tool that motivates students to take action on feedback. *Australasian Journal of Engineering Education, 20*(1), 9–18.

Johnston-Wilder, S., & Lee, C. (2010). Mathematical resilience. *Mathematics Teaching,* (218), 38–41.

Jong, M. S.-Y., & Shang, J. (2015). Impeding phenomena emerging from students' constructivist online game-based learning process: Implications for the importance of teacher facilitation. *Journal of Educational Technology and Society, 18*(2), 262–283.

Kale, U., & Goh, D. (2014). Teaching style, ICT experience and teachers' attitudes toward teaching with web 2.0. *Education and Information Technologies, 19*(1), 41–60.

Kang, M., & Im, T. (2013). Factors of learner–instructor interaction which predict perceived learning outcomes in online learning environment. *Journal of Computer Assisted Learning, 29*(3), 292–301.

Kapp, K. M. (2012). *The gamification of learning and instruction: Game-based methods and strategies for training and education.* San Francisco: Wiley.

Kay, R. (2006). Using asynchronous online discussion to learn introductory programming: An exploratory analysis. *Canadian Journal of Learning and Technology, 32*(1).

Kaymak, Z. D., & Horzum, M. B. (2013). Relationship between online learning readiness and structure and interaction of online learning students. *Educational Sciences: Theory and Practice, 13*(3), 1792–1797.

Kearns, L. R., & Frey, B. A. (2010). Web 2.0 technologies and back channel communication in an online learning community. *TechTrends: Linking Research and Practice to Improve Learning, 54*(4), 41–51.

Keengwe, J., Adjei-Boateng, E., & Diteeyont, W. (2013). Facilitating active social presence and meaningful interactions in online learning. *Education Information Technology, 18*(4), 597–607.

Keengwe, J., Schnellert, G., & Jonas, D. (2014). Mobile phones in education: Challenges and opportunities for learning. *Education and Information Technologies, 19*(2), 441–450.

Kelleher, J. (2015). Create a sense of urgency to spark learning. *Phi Delta Kappan, 97*(2), 21–26.

Keller, T. E., Whitaker, J. K., & Burke, T. K. (2001). Student debates in policy courses: Promoting practice skills and knowledge through active learning. *Journal of Social Work Education, 37*(2), 343–351.

Kemp, W. C. (2002). Persistence of adult learners in distance education. *American Journal of Distance Education, 16*(2), 65–81.

Kena, G., Aud, S., Johnson, F., Wang, X., Zhang, J., Rathbun, A., . . . Kristapovich, P. (2014). *The condition of education 2014* (NCES 2014–083). Washington, DC: U.S. Department of Education, National Center for Education Statistics. Accessed at http://nces.ed.gov/pubs2014/2014083.pdf on July 7, 2016.

Kena, G., Hussar, W., McFarland, J., de Brey, C., & Musu-Gillette, L. (2016). *The condition of education 2016* (NCES 2016-144). Washington, DC: U.S. Department of Education, National Center for Education Statistics. Accessed at http://nces.ed.gov/pubs2016/2016144.pdf on July 7, 2016.

Kentnor, H. E. (2015). Distance education and the evolution of online learning in the United States. *Curriculum and Teaching Dialogue, 17*(1/2), 21–34.

Kerawalla, L., Littleton, K., Scanlon, E., Jones, A., Gaved, M., Collins, T., . . . Petrou, M. (2013). Personal inquiry learning trajectories in geography: Technological support across contexts. *Interactive Learning Environments, 21*(6), 497–515.

Kincaid, K., & Pfau, P. (2015). Creating ever-evolving, school-specific learning commons. *Teacher Librarian, 42*(4), 8–14.

Kinchin, I. (2012). Avoiding technology-enhanced non-learning. *British Journal of Educational Technology, 43*(2), E43–E48.

King-Sears, M. E. (2007). Designing and delivering learning center instruction. *Intervention in School and Clinic, 42*(3), 137–147.

Klein, C. (2014). The brain at rest: What it is doing and why that matters. *Philosophy of Science*, *81*(5), 974–985.

Kolb, D. A. (1984). *Experiential learning: Experience as the source of learning and development.* Englewood Cliffs, NJ: Prentice Hall.

Kong, S. C., Chan, T.-W., Griffin, P., Hoppe, U., Huang, R., Kinshuk, C. K. L., et al. (2014). E-learning in school education in the coming 10 years for developing 21st century skills: Critical research issues and policy implications. *Journal of Educational Technology and Society*, *17*(1), 70–78.

Koszalka, T. A., & Ntloedibe-Kuswani, G. S. (2010). Literature on the safe and disruptive learning potential of mobile technologies. *Distance Education*, *31*(2), 139–157.

Koutsabasis, P., Stavrakis, M., Spyrou, T., & Darzentas, J. (2011). Perceived impact of asynchronous e-learning after long-term use: Implications for design and development. *International Journal of Human-Computer Interaction*, *27*(2), 191–213.

Kožuh, I., Jeremić, Z., Sarjaš, A., Bele, J. L., Devedžić, V., & Debevc, M. (2015). Social presence and interaction in learning environments: The effect on student success. *Journal of Educational Technology and Society*, *18*(1), 223–236.

Lai, K., Khaddage, F., & Knezek, G. (2013). Blending student technology experiences in formal and informal learning. *Journal of Computer Assisted Learning*, *29*(5), 414–425.

Lally, V., Sharples, M., Tracy, F., Bertram, N., & Masters, S. (2012). Researching the ethical dimensions of mobile, ubiquitous and immersive technology enhanced learning (MUITEL): A thematic review and dialogue. *Interactive Learning Environments*, *20*(3), 217–238.

Lawes, C. J. (2015). Talking less but saying more: Teaching U.S. history online. *Journal of American History*, *101*(4), 1204–1214.

Lee, C.-Y. (2015). Changes in self-efficacy and task value in online learning. *Distance Education*, *36*(1), 59–79.

Lee, E., Pate, J. A., & Cozart, D. (2015). Autonomy support for online students. *TechTrends: Linking Research and Practice to Improve Learning*, *59*(4), 54–61.

Lee, J. K., & Lee, W. K. (2008). The relationship of e-learner's self-regulatory efficacy and perception of e-learning environmental quality. *Computers in Human Behavior*, *24*(1), 32–47.

Lee, S. W., O'Doherty, J. P., & Shimojo, S. (2015). Neural computations mediating one-shot learning in the human brain. *Plos Biology*, *13*(4), 1–36.

Lee, Y., & Choi, J. (2011). A review of online course dropout research: Implications for practice and future research. *Educational Technology Research and Development*, *59*(5), 593–618.

Li, C. (2010). *Open leadership: How social technology can transform the way you lead.* San Francisco: Jossey-Bass.

Li, S. C., & Choi, T. H. (2014). Does social capital matter? A quantitative approach to examining technology infusion in schools. *Journal of Computer Assisted Learning, 30*(1), 1–16.

Linder-VanBerschot, J. A., & Summers, L. L. (2015). Designing instruction in the face of technology transience. *Quarterly Review of Distance Education, 16*(2), 107–118.

Lippman, P. C. (2015). Designing collaborative spaces for schools. *Education Digest, 80*(5), 39–44.

Liu, T.-C., Lin, Y.-C., & Paas, F. (2014). Effects of prior knowledge on learning from different compositions of representations in a mobile learning environment. *Computer Education, 72,* 328–338.

López-Pérez, M. V., Pérez-López, M. C., Rodríguez-Ariza, L., & Argente-Linares, E. (2013). The influence of the use of technology on student outcomes in a blended learning context. *Educational Technology Research and Development, 61*(4), 625–638.

Lu, J., & Law, N. Y. (2012). Understanding collaborative learning behavior from Moodle log data. *Interactive Learning Environments, 20*(5), 451–466.

Macfadyen, L. P., & Dawson, S. (2010). Mining LMS data to develop an "early warning system" for educators: A proof of concept. *Computers and Education, 54*(2), 588–599.

Magistro, D., Takeuchi, H., Nejad, K. K., Taki, Y., Sekiguchi, A., Nouchi, R., et al.. (2015). The relationship between processing speed and regional white matter volume in healthy young people. *Plos ONE, 10*(9), 1–17.

Manning, S., Stanford, B., & Reeves, S. (2010). Valuing the advanced learner: Differentiating up. *The Clearing House, 83*(4), 145–149.

Mao, J., & Peck, K. (2013). Assessment strategies, self-regulated learning skills, and perceptions of assessment in online learning. *Quarterly Review of Distance Education, 14*(2), 75–95.

Marzano, R. J., & Haystead, M. W. (2008). *Making standards useful in the classroom.* Alexandria, VA: Association for Supervision and Curriculum Development.

Marzano, R. J., Warrick, P., & Simms, J. A. (2014). *A handbook for high reliability schools: The next step in school reform.* Bloomington, IN: Marzano Research.

Mayer, R. E. (Ed.). (2005). *Cambridge handbook of multimedia learning.* New York: Cambridge University Press.

Mayes, R., Luebeck, J., Ku, H.-Y., Akarasriworn, C., & Korkmaz, Ö. (2011). Themes and strategies for transformative online instruction: A review of literature and practice. *Quarterly Review of Distance Education, 12*(3), 151–166.

Mazzolini, M., & Maddison, S. (2007). When to jump in: The role of the instructor in online discussion forums. *Computers and Education, 49*(2), 193–213.

Means, B., Bakia, M., & Murphy, R. (2015). *Learning online: What research tells us about whether, when, and how.* New York: Routledge.

Miller, D. L. (2013). Got it wrong? Think again. And again. *Phi Delta Kappan, 94*(5), 50–52.

Miller, G. A. (1956). The magical number seven, plus or minus two: Some limits on our capacity for processing information. *Psychological Review, 63,* 81–97.

Min, J., & Wu, Y.-S. (2012). Development of a web-based system to support self-directed learning of microfabrication technologies. *Journal of Educational Technology and Society, 15*(4), 205–213.

Moallem, M. (2015). The impact of synchronous and asynchronous communication tools on learner self-regulation, social presence, immediacy, intimacy, and satisfaction in collaborative online learning. *The Online Journal of Distance Education and e-Learning, 3*(3), 55–77.

Molnar, A. (Ed.). (2015). *Virtual schools in the U.S. 2015: Politics, performance, policy, and research evidence.* Boulder, CO: National Education Policy Center.

Moreillon, J. (2015). Increasing interactivity in the online learning environment: Using digital tools to support students in socially constructed meaning-making. *TechTrends: Linking Research and Practice to Improve Learning, 59*(3), 41–47.

Mostert, M., & Snowball, J. D. (2013). Where angels fear to tread: Online peer-assessment in a large first-year class. *Assessment and Evaluation in Higher Education, 38*(6), 674–686.

Müller, T. (2008). Persistence of women in online degree-completion programs. *International Review of Research in Open and Distance Learning, 9,* 1–18.

Multisilta, J. (2013). Mobile panoramic video applications for learning. *Education and Information Technologies, 19*(3), 655–666.

Myers, S. A., & Thorn, K. (2013). The relationship between students' motives to communicate with their instructors, course effort, and course workload. *College Student Journal, 47*(3), 485–488.

Nandi, D., Hamilton, M., & Harland, J. (2012). Evaluating the quality of interaction in asynchronous discussion forums in fully online courses. *Distance Education, 33*(1), 5–30.

National Alliance for Public Charter Schools. (2016, June). A call to action to improve the quality of full-time virtual charter public schools. Accessed at www.publiccharters.org /wp-content/uploads/2016/06/Virtuals-FINAL-06202016-1.pdf on October 27, 2016.

Newkirk, T. (2012). *The art of slow reading: Six time-honored practices for engagement.* Portsmouth, NH: Heinemann.

Nonnecke, B., & Preece, J. (2000, April). *Lurker demographics: Counting the silent.* Paper presented at the Proceedings of CHI 2000, The Hague, Netherlands.

Olson, J., & Knott, L. (2013). When a problem is more than a teacher's question. *Educational Studies in Mathematics, 83*(1), 27–36.

Oztok, M., Zingaro, D., Brett, C., & Hewitt, J. (2013). Exploring asynchronous and synchronous tool use in online courses. *Computers and Education, 60*(1), 87–94.

Paas, F., & Ayres, P. (2014). Cognitive load theory: A broader view on the role of memory in learning and education. *Educational Psychology Review, 26*(2), 191–195.

Park, H., & Seo, S. (2013). Effects of collaborative activities on group identity in virtual world. *Interactive Learning Environments, 21*(6), 516–527.

Park, J.-H., & Choi, H. J. (2009). Factors influencing adult learners' decision to drop out or persist in online learning. *Journal of Educational Technology and Society, 12*(4), 207–217.

Parkin, H. J., Hepplestone, S., Holden, G., Irwin, B., & Thorpe, L. (2012). A role for technology in enhancing students' engagement with feedback. *Assessment and Evaluation in Higher Education, 37*(8), 963–973.

Pauli, R., Mohiyeddini, C., Bray, D., Michie, F., & Street, B. (2008). Individual differences in negative group work experiences in collaborative student learning. *Educational Psychology, 28*(1), 47–58.

Pearcy, M. (2014). Student, teacher, professor: Three perspectives on online education. *History Teacher, 47*(2), 169–185.

Pekrun, R., Goetz, T., Frenzel, A. C., Barchfeld, P., & Perry, R. P. (2011). Measuring emotions in students' learning and performance: The achievement emotions questionnaire (AEQ). *Contemporary Educational Psychology, 36*(1), 36–48.

Perkins, S. (2015). Studying? Don't answer that text! *Science News, 187*(13), 29.

Perry, E. H., & Pilati, M. L. (2011). Online learning. *New Directions for Teaching and Learning, 2011*(128), 95–104.

Picciano, A. G., & Seaman, J. (2009). *K–12 online learning: A 2008 follow-up of the survey of U.S. school district administrators*. Needham, MA: The Sloan Consortium.

Piccoli, G., Ahmad, R., & Ives, B. (2001). Web-based virtual learning environments: A research framework and a preliminary assessment of effectiveness in basic IT skills training. *MIS Quarterly, 25*(4), 401–426.

Pintrich, P. R. (2004). A conceptual framework for assessing motivation and self-regulated learning in college students. *Educational Psychology Review, 16*(4), 385–407.

Poole, A. (2011). The online reading strategies used by five successful Taiwanese ESL learners. *Asian Anthropology, 10*, 65–87.

Powell, A., Roberts, V., & Patrick, S. (2015). *Using online learning for credit recovery: Getting back on track to graduation*. Vienna, VA: The International Association for K–12 Online Learning.

Quinlan, A. (2011). 12 tips for the online teacher. *Phi Delta Kappan, 92*(4), 28–31.

Raywid, M. A. (1999). History and issues of alternative schools. *Education Digest, 64*(9), 47–51.

Reason, L., Boyd, M., & Reason, C. (2016). Cyberbullying in rural communities: Origin and processing through the lens of older adolescents. *The Qualitative Report, 21*(12), 2331–2348.

Redding, A. B., James, C., & Gardner, H. (2016). Nurturing ethical collaboration. *Independent School, 75*(2), 58–64.

Reilly, J. R., Gallagher-Lepak, S., & Killion, C. (2012). "Me and my computer": Emotional factors in online learning. *Nursing Education Perspectives, 33*(2), 100–105.

Resta, P., & Laferriere, T. (2007). Technology in support of collaborative learning. *Educational Psychology Review, 19*(1), 65–83.

Richardson, J. C., & Swan, K. (2003). Examining social presence in online courses in relation to students' perceived learning and satisfaction. *Journal of Asynchronous Learning Networks, 7*(1), 68–88.

Rogerson-Revell, P. (2015). Constructively aligning technologies with learning and assessment in a distance education master's programme. *Distance Education, 36*(1), 129–147.

Rogo, E. J., & Portillo, K. M. (2015). E-model for online learning communities. *Journal of Dental Hygiene, 89*(5), 293–304.

Roschelle, J., Rafanan, K., Bhanot, R., Estrella, G., Penuel, B., Nussbaum, M., et al. (2010). Scaffolding group explanation and feedback with handheld technology: Impact on students' mathematics learning. *Educational Technology Research and Development, 58*(4), 399–419.

Rosenberg, M. J. (2000). *E-learning: Strategies for delivering knowledge in the digital age.* Columbus, OH: McGraw-Hill.

Salomon, G., & Globerson, T. (1989). When teams do not function the way they ought to. *International Journal of Educational Research 13*(1), 89–99.

Schank, R. C., Fano, A., Bell, B., & Jona, M. (1994). The design of goal-based scenarios. *Journal of the Learning Sciences, 3*(4), 305–345.

Schellens, T., & Valcke, M. (2006). Fostering knowledge construction in university students through asynchronous discussion groups. *Computers and Education, 46*(4), 349–370.

Schreiner, L. A. (2010). Thriving in the classroom. *About Campus, 15*(3), 2–10.

Seiver, J. G., & Troja, A. (2014). Satisfaction and success in online learning as a function of the needs for affiliation, autonomy, and mastery. *Distance Education, 35*(1), 90–105.

Sekeres, D. C., Coiro, J., Castek, J., & Guzniczak, L. A. (2014). Wondering + online inquiry = learning. *Phi Delta Kappan, 96*(3), 44–48.

Selwyn, N. (2011). Digitally distanced learning: A study of international distance learners' (non)use of technology. *Distance Education, 32*(1), 85–99.

Shadiev, R., Hwang, W.-Y., Chen, N.-S., & Huang, Y.-M. (2014). Review of speech-to-text recognition technology for enhancing learning. *Journal of Educational Technology and Society, 17*(4), 65–84.

Shea, P., Victers, J., & Hayes, S. (2010). Online instructional effort measured through the lens of teaching presence in the community of inquiry framework: A re-examination of measures and approach. *International Review of Research in Open and Distance Learning, 11*(3), 127–154.

Shin, N., Sutherland, L. M., Norris, C. A., & Soloway, E. (2012). Effects of game technology on elementary student learning in mathematics. *British Journal of Educational Technology, 43*(4), 540–560.

Short, J., Williams, E., & Christie, B. (1976). *The social psychology of telecommunications.* London: Wiley.

Slavich, G., & Zimbardo, P. (2012). Transformational teaching: Theoretical underpinnings, basic principles, and core methods. *Educational Psychology Review, 24*(4), 569–608.

Smith, S. J., & Basham, J. D. (2014). Designing online learning opportunities for students with disabilities. *Teaching Exceptional Children, 46*(5), 127–137.

Snyder, T. D., de Brey, C., & Dillow, S. (2016). *Digest of education statistics 2014* (50th ed.). Washington, DC: U.S. Department of Education. Retrieved from http://nces.ed.gov/pubs2016/2016006.pdf on October 27, 2016.

Snyder, K. E., & Linnenbrink-Garcia, L. (2013). A developmental, person-centered approach to exploring multiple motivational pathways in gifted underachievement. *Educational Psychologist, 48*(4), 209–228.

Song, Y., Wong, L.-H., & Looi, C.-K. (2012). Fostering personalized learning in science inquiry supported by mobile technologies. *Educational Technology Research and Development, 60*(4), 679–701.

Sparks, S. D. (2015). In math, positive mindset may prime students' brains. *Education Week, 35*(14), 6.

Spector, J. M. (2013). Emerging educational technologies and research directions. *Journal of Educational Technology and Society, 16*(2), 21–30.

Stanley, D. (2013). Can technology improve large class learning? The case of an upper-division business core class. *Journal of Education for Business, 88*(5), 265–270.

Steiner, G. (2009). Forgetting while learning: A plea for specific consolidation. *Journal of Cognitive Education and Psychology, 8*(2), 117–127.

Stone, A. (2014). Online assessment: What influences students to engage with feedback? *Clinical Teacher, 11*(4), 284–289.

Strauss, V. (2016, February 10). The education mess in Ohio under Gov. John Kasich. *Washington Post.* Accessed at www.washingtonpost.com/news/answer-sheet/wp/2016/02/10/the-education-mess-in-ohio-under-gov-john-kasich on March 3, 2016.

Student takes: How does technology improve learning? (2015). *Educational Leadership, 72*(8), 92–93.

Sugar, W., & van Tryon, P. J. S. (2014). Development of a virtual technology coach to support technology integration for K–12 educators. *TechTrends: Linking Research and Practice to Improve Learning, 58*(3), 54–62.

Sullivan, P. (2011). Professor's page: *Asking students harder questions. Australian Primary Mathematics Classroom, 16*(4), 17–18.

Summers, J. J., & Svinicki, M. D. (2007). Investigating classroom community in higher education supported by mobile technologies. *Education Technology Research Development, 60,* 679–701.

Swan, B., Coulombe-Quach, X., Huang, A., Godek, J., Becker, D., & Zhou, Y. (2015). Meeting the needs of gifted and talented students. *Journal of Advanced Academics, 26*(4), 294–319.

Swan, K., Shea, P., Richardson, J., Ice, P., Garrison, D. R., Cleveland-Innes, M., et al. (2008). Validating a measurement tool of presence in online communities of inquiry. *E-Mentor, 2*(24), 1–12.

Terrion, J., & Aceti, V. (2012). Perceptions of the effects of clicker technology on student learning and engagement: A study of freshman chemistry students. *Research in Learning Technology, 20*(2), 1–11.

Thomas, T. A. (2014). Developing team skills through a collaborative writing assignment. *Assessment and Evaluation in Higher Education, 39*(4), 479–495.

Tobin, T. J. (2014). Increase online student retention with universal design for learning. *Quarterly Review of Distance Education, 15*(3), 13–24.

Todhunter, B. (2013). LOL—limitations of online learning—are we selling the open and distance education message short? *Distance Education, 34*(2), 232–252.

Tseng, H., Ku, H.-Y., Wang, C.-H., & Sun, L. (2009). Key factors in online collaboration and their relationship to teamwork satisfaction. *Quarterly Review of Distance Education, 10*(2), 195–206.

Tu, C. H., & Corry, M. (2002). Research in online learning community. *Journal of Instructional Science and Technology, 5*(1).

Tu, C.-H., Sujo-Montes, L., Yen, C.-J., Chan, J.-Y., & Blocher, M. (2012). The integration of personal learning environments & open network learning environments. *TechTrends: Linking Research and Practice to Improve Learning, 56*(3), 13–19.

Tucker, B. (2014). Student evaluation surveys: Anonymous comments that offend or are unprofessional. *Higher Education, 68*(3), 347–358.

Tucker, R., & Abbasi, N. (2015). The architecture of teamwork: Examining relationships between teaching, assessment, student learning and satisfaction with creative design outcomes. *Architectural Engineering and Design Management, 11*(6), 405–422.

Vadeboncoeur, J., Alkouatli, C., & Amini, N. (2015). Elaborating "dialogue" in communities of inquiry: Attention to discourse as a method for facilitating dialogue across difference. *Childhood and Philosophy*, *11*(22), 299–318.

Vazquez-Cano, E. (2014). Mobile distance learning with smartphones and apps in higher education. *Educational Sciences: Theory and Practice*, *14*(5), 1505–1520.

Verbert, K., Manouselis, N., Drachsler, H., & Duval, E. (2012). Dataset-driven research to support learning and knowledge analytics. *Journal of Educational Technology and Society*, *15*(3), 133–148.

Vess, D. (2004). History in the digital age: A study of the impact of interactive resources on student learning. *History Teacher*, *37*(3), 385–399.

Visser-Wijnveen, G. J., Stes, A., Van Petegem, P. (2014). Clustering teachers' motivations for teaching. *Teaching in Higher Education*, *19*(6), 644–656.

Vo, H. X., & Morris, R. L. (2006). Debate as a tool in teaching economics: Rationale, technique, and some evidence. *Journal of Education for Business*, *81*(6), 315–320.

Vonderwell, S. K., & Boboc, M. (2013). Promoting formative assessment in online teaching and learning. *TechTrends: Linking Research and Practice to Improve Learning*, *57*(4), 22–27.

Wan, N. (2011). Why digital literacy is important for science teaching and learning. *Teaching Science: The Journal of the Australian Science Teachers Association*, *57*(4), 26–32.

Wang, C.-H., Shannon, D. M., & Ross, M. E. (2013). Students' characteristics, self-regulated learning, technology self-efficacy, and course outcomes in online learning. *Distance Education*, *34*(3), 302–323.

Wang, F., & Burton, J. K. (2010). Collaborative learning problems and identity salience: A mixed methods study. *Journal of Educational Technology Development and Exchange*, *3*(1), 1–12.

Wang, Y., Han, X., & Yang, J. (2015). Revisiting the blended learning literature: Using a complex adaptive systems framework. *Journal of Educational Technology and Society*, *18*(2), 380–393.

Waters, L. H., Barbour, M. K., & Menchaca, M. P. (2014). The nature of online charter schools: Evolution and emerging concerns. *Journal of Educational Technology and Society*, *17*(4), 379–389.

Watson, A. C., Wirtz, M., & Sumpter, L. (2015). Putting memory to work. *Independent School*, *75*(1), 56–60.

Watson, J., Pape, L., Murin, A., Gemin, B., & Vashaw, L. (2014). *Keeping pace with K–12 digital learning: An annual review of policy and practice* (11th ed.). Mountain View, CA: Creative Commons.

Web Accessibility Initiative. (2012, October). *Web content accessibility guidelines (WCAG) overview*. Accessed at www.w3.org/WAI/intro/wcag on July 7, 2016.

Wei, C.-W., & Chen, N.-S. (2012). A model for social presence in online classrooms. *Educational Technology Research and Development*, *60*(3), 529–545.

Wieth, M. B., & Burns, B. D. (2014). Rewarding multitasking: Negative effects of an incentive on problem solving under divided attention. *Journal of Problem Solving, 7*(1), 60–72.

Williams, S. S., Jaramillo, A., & Pesko, J. C. (2015). Improving depth of thinking in online discussion boards. *Quarterly Review of Distance Education, 16*(3), 45–66.

Witteveen, A. (2015). Better together. *Library Journal, 140*(20), 42–44.

Wojtowicz, M., Day, V., McGrath, P. J., & Eysenbach, G. (2013). Predictors of participant retention in a guided online self-help program for university students: Prospective cohort study. *Journal of Medical Internet Research, 15*(5).

Woolley, A. W., Hackman, R. R., Jerde, T. E., Chabris, C. F., Bennett, S. L., & Kosslyn, S. M. (2007). Using brain-based measures to compose teams: How individual capabilities and team collaboration strategies jointly shape performance. *Social Neuroscience, 2*(2), 96–105.

Wright, P. (2014). "E-tivities from the front line": A community of inquiry case study analysis of educators' blog posts on the topic of designing and delivering online learning. *Education Sciences, 4*(2), 172–192.

Wu, J.-W., Tseng, J. C. R., & Hwang, G.-J. (2015). Development of an inquiry-based learning support system based on an intelligent knowledge exploration approach. *Journal of Educational Technology and Society, 18*(3), 282–300.

Young, M. (2010). The art and science of fostering engaged learning. *Academy of Educational Leadership Journal, 14*, 1–18.

Yuan, J., & Kim, C. (2014). Guidelines for facilitating the development of learning communities in online courses. *Journal of Computer Assisted Learning, 30*(3), 220–232.

YunJeong, C., & Hannafin, M. J. (2015). The uses (and misuses) of collaborative distance education technologies. *Quarterly Review of Distance Education, 16*(2), 77–92.

Zhu, E. (2006). Interaction and cognitive engagement: An analysis of four asynchronous online discussions. *Instructional Science, 34*, 451–480.

Zimmerman, B. J., & Schunk, D. H. (2011). Self-regulated learning and performance: An introduction and an overview. In B. J. Zimmerman & D. H. Schunk (Eds.), *Handbook of self-regulation of learning and performance* (pp. 1–12). New York: Routledge.

Zydney, J. M., & Hasselbring, T. S. (2014). Mini anchors: A universal design for learning approach. *TechTrends: Linking Research and Practice to Improve Learning, 58*(6), 21–28.

Index

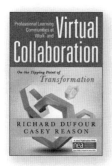

Professional Learning Communities at Work™ and Virtual Collaboration
Richard DuFour and Casey Reason
Learn how to combine the capacities of the PLC at Work™ process and powerful technology tools to transform teaching and learning. Realize the potential of virtual collaboration to support the PLC process, and discover research-based strategies for reaching sustained levels of deeper learning.
BKF673

Solutions for Digital Learner–Centered Classrooms series
Gain practical, high-impact strategies to enhance instruction and heighten student achievement in 21st century classrooms. Using tech-based tools and techniques, your staff will discover how to motivate students to develop curiosity, become actively engaged, and have a sense of purpose in their education.
KTF198, BKF691, BKF680, BKF636, BKF679, BKF681, BKF664, BKF666

From Pencils to Podcasts
Katie Stover and Lindsay Yearta
This practical resource provides K–6 teachers with suggestions for incorporating technology into familiar literacy practices and illustrates ways technology can deepen students' literacy development. Each chapter includes information about easy-to-use technology tools, examples from real classrooms, and step-by-step instructions to get started.
BKF689

Bring Your Own Device
Kipp D. Rogers
This book shows educators how to incorporate students' personal technology tools into instruction. BYOD allows students to be active participants in their learning and helps teachers equip them with the skills required to be college, career, and citizenship ready.
BKF672

Solution Tree | Press
a division of
Solution Tree

Visit SolutionTree.com or call 800.733.6786 to order.

Wait! Your professional development journey doesn't have to end with the last pages of this book.

We realize improving student learning doesn't happen overnight. And your school or district shouldn't be left to puzzle out all the details of this process alone.

No matter where you are on the journey, we're committed to helping you get to the next stage.

Take advantage of everything from **custom workshops** to **keynote presentations** and **interactive web and video conferencing**. We can even help you develop an action plan tailored to fit your specific needs.

Let's get the conversation started.

Call 888.763.9045 today.

SolutionTree.com